Blessings as you
read This
Miriam Neff

FROM
ONE WIDOW
TO ANOTHER

MIRIAM NEFF

FROM ONE WIDOW TO ANOTHER

Conversations on the New You

MOODY PUBLISHERS
Chicago

All Scripture quotations, unless otherwise indicated, are taken from the Holy Bible, New International Version". NIV". Copyright © 1973, 1978, 1984 by International Bible Society. Used by permission of Zondervan. All rights reserved.

Scripture quotations marked NASB are taken from the New American Standard Bible®, Copyright © 1960, 1962, 1963, 1968, 1971, 1972, 1973, 1975, 1977, 1995 by The Lockman Foundation. Used by permission. (www. Lockman.org)

Scripture quotations marked NRSV are from the New Revised Standard Version Bible, copyright © 1989 National Council of the Churches of Christ in the United States of America. Used by permission. All rights reserved.

Scripture quotations marked CEV are taken from the Contemporary English Version. Copyright © 1991, 1992, 1995 by American Bible Society. Used by permission.

Emphases in Scripture verses are the author's. Some Scripture references are written with feminine wording for readability.

All Web sites listed herein are accurate at the time of publication but may change in the future or cease to exist. The citing of Web sites or other references does not imply publisher endorsement of the entire contents.

Editor: Pam Pugh
Interior Design: Ragont Design
Cover Design: LeVan Fisher Design

Library of Congress Cataloging-in-Publication Data

Neff, Miriam.
From one widow to another : conversations on the new you / Miriam Neff.
    p. cm.
Includes bibliographical references.
ISBN 978-0-8024-8784-1
1. Widows—Religious life. I. Title.
BV4528.N44 2009
248.8'434—dc22
                    2008029224

We hope you enjoy this book from Moody Publishers. Our goal is to provide high-quality, thought-provoking books and products that connect truth to your real needs and challenges. For more information on other books and products written and produced from a biblical perspective, go to www. moodypublishers.com or write to:

Moody Publishers
820 N. LaSalle Boulevard
Chicago, IL 60610

3 5 7 9 10 8 6 4 2

Printed in the United States of America

*I*n 1979 I dedicated my first book "To my husband, Bob, the most Christlike person I know."

In 1992 I dedicated my third book "To Bob, for twenty years of shared parenting and twenty-seven years of unconditional commitment. I recently asked him how our life compared to what he had anticipated on our first date, an outing back in 1963 on a beautiful fall day in Brown County, Indiana. He answered, 'The challenges and adventure are more than I ever dreamed.' This book is the result of both, and this working mom could not have written it without his incredible, ever-believing support."

On April 21, 2006, I experienced the third greatest event in my life: Bob's exit to heaven. Following my choice to marry him, then his impact on my choosing to be a Christ follower, his exit was profound, far beyond the words that have resulted in this book.

After forty-one years of marriage, family, babies, adoption, careers, crises in the lives of those we cherished most, moving, ministries, traveling the world together—Alaska to Albania, Maine to Morocco, Romania to Russia—the world shrunk in my view; the man grew in my love and esteem. Our final journey through the months and years of amyotrophic lateral sclerosis was the greatest, and toughest, though most precious of them all.

Today, my dedication again is "to my husband, Bob, *still* the most Christlike person I have ever known."

—Miriam Neff

CONTENTS

ACKNOWLEDGMENTS

*R*eal living is a team event. This last challenge has required more emotional stamina, physical strength, spiritual courage, and mental resolve than I possess. My team is composed of cherished familiar faces and surprises as well.

First, my children have rallied with strength I did not know they possessed, sacrificing more than I can imagine of their own lives, career paths, and pleasures, to carry their Dad and me through.

Valerie and husband, Mark Hogan, what pillars of strength and persistence through the hardest of times! And today, thank you, Valerie, for pressing me to begin Widow Connection on my own. And Mark, for being such capable eyes, ears, and wisdom in my new life without Bob. And all this with parenting, law school, coaching, school board meetings, and work. What big hearts you have!

John and Lori, your dependability wrapped in creativity and care bless me today. John, my new ministry would not exist without you, your technical skills, and patience. Lori, you are like Dad, positive, smiling, and always expecting the best will happen.

Charles, Mr. Fix-It, you literally lifted your Dad day after day, month after month. Moving home and meeting the challenge was the greatest gift you could have given him.

Rob, our grill master, Bob's face lit up when you entered the room. You brought your philosophy of life to us when we needed it most. You always said, "We don't need a reason to be happy." Strong and tender, we needed your perspective.

Grandchildren Edward, Albert, and Edmond, no one brought

more excitement, laughter, and delightful unexpected moments to
Bob like the three of you did. Edward, you were Grandpa's hands in
assembling and repairs. Albert, Bob loved to hear you read aloud.
Whether *Calvin and Hobbes*, or hearing you laugh, he loved it! Edmond, coming to the family late (as all of you did), you told your
coach that you did not have a Grandpa long enough. Please know,
he, too, wanted more time with you. He loved you all so much.

And my small and tenacious group of friends, whose stories
are scattered through these pages—I may have changed your
names, but you'll be recognized in heaven. Leaders in our widows
group at church, my board for Widow Connection, and the widows and widowers who have sent thanks, encouragement, and your
stories to Widowconnection.com, you have carried me on your
shoulders when my heart wanted to hide under the bench on the
sidelines.

Thanks to the Gibbs, Milne, and Warton families for providing
me with your get-away homes for rest and reflection. You have re-
stored my soul.

And, of course, Moody Publishers, Greg Thornton, Jennifer
Lyell, and Pam Pugh—without you, this book would not exist.

I thank God for all of you.

—Miriam Neff

INTRODUCTION

*I*magine a single event that will dramatically change your calendar, your checkbook, your friendship network, the contents of your refrigerator, the temperature you set your thermostat, your outlook on your future, and your connection with your children. And that's not all. Your appearance may change, your emotions, your sleep patterns, your theology, your social status, and possibly your address.

I experienced most of these changes and more beginning on April 21, 2006—the day I became a widow. I don't like the word and still will not check that box to identify myself. Turning points in life such as deciding to marry, divorce, become a parent, find a career—all these events are accompanied by large changes. The difference in these is that *we chose* them. But becoming a widow *happens*. Many of the changes in my life were surprises and many were not pleasant. But here I am. Perhaps you too have joined this elite club of widowhood, one we did not choose to belong to. Yet here it is where we find comfort from those who embarked on this journey before we did. They understand the feeling that half of ourselves has been torn away. The wound is large and we question whether we will heal, and, if so, when?

You and I are not alone. Eight hundred thousand people join our ranks in the United States annually.[1] We are one of the fastest growing demographics.

I attempted in those first months to find help, to discover resources, to find information, relevant advice, and comfort. I browsed the library checking out armloads of books and wandered through bookstores. I searched the Internet (which is conveniently available 24/7 with my new sleep pattern). Yes, there were good books on grieving and on financial advice. But I did not find a comprehensive book for widows with a spiritual perspective.

Trips to Ghana and Burkina Faso in Africa, to the Dominican Republic, and a poignant return to National Religious Broadcasters that first year turned my attention from my past to an unknown future.

When I was in the widows village in Africa, what initiated my resolve to provide a resource for other widows? Was it the hunger in their eyes? Was it their desire to learn and help each other? Was it the recognition of the cross-cultural message of the biblical widow and her pot of oil? Was it my catamaran adventure? Maybe it was my discovery that, with all our wealth of knowledge and resources, we've missed something here in our culture. With a surprising sense of clarity and focus, I decided to create such a resource. This book is a significant part of that.

May I first talk about our vulnerabilities? Within days of Bob's exit to heaven, I became aware of my vulnerability. While the first "in my face" experience was related to finances, many more were to follow, heightened by the intensity of grief. Emotions with the intensity of Hurricane Katrina create a window in our lives where clear thinking is absent. Yes, in this world there are others who will take advantage of that, but we can be our own enemy as well.

As surely as *vulnerable* describes us, so does *strength*. Look with me at our new boldness, our new freedom and flexibility, and our new ability to comfort others. We are forced to change because the world as we knew it shifted dramatically. Because the human spirit strives to rise and move forward, we have to reach for resources we never knew we had, skills within that had never been needed, and hope within, in order to face each new day. We catch a glimpse of the new person in the mirror and whisper to her, "I didn't know you could."

Every relationship we have is affected by our loss. When we and our husband got married, the two of us became one. Now we have been ripped in two parts again, and it's as though half of us no longer exists. I stood in front of Bob's colleagues to bring a devotional one year after becoming a widow. I began by saying, "I'm half here!" This statement sounds strange, and some of their faces mirrored that. But the feeling is quite real.

Every person in our life is affected by the reality of the different/ new person we are. My personal changes were a great surprise to me! Some need to abandon that person. For all who stay, a new bond must be created because the old one is gone. For all who stay in my friendship circle, a new bond must be created with the new Miriam. In a kaleidoscope, one tiny rock shifts and the pattern moves. Every "rock" of us has shifted. It is as if half the essence of our being changes. No wonder the reality of who we now are may bear little resemblance to who we were in our marriage. Looking at friends and family in light of this truth helps us face why our network shrinks—and it also frees us to relate in new ways to those who are still in our life.

Kind friends saw me floundering in the grayness after Bob's exit to heaven. I felt I knew nothing of who Miriam was. "What were you like before you met Bob?" some asked. I was a seventeen-year-old Indiana University freshman trying to find my way to a 7:30 a.m. chemistry lab on the opposite side of campus from Teter Quad. Not much of a firm identity going on there! While most do not marry as early as I (at age nineteen), and do much of their growing up after marriage, I discovered that most women, on becoming widowed, struggle with finding their role and their worth. We will look at the new person we can become. While finding ourselves again is essential, finding a mission, a purpose in life, becomes necessary as well.

I believe no one goes through this experience without a profound spiritual impact. We are more than mind, body, and emotions. Facing death grabs our soul and shakes it. What happens next? What of life's investments were worth the price? worth the sacrifice? I have been privileged to meet some widows who discovered their Creator in a personal way *because* of their loss. I prayed as another discovered her Maker in our widows group. A time of crisis is another opportunity for every human to examine that spiritual void, and choose to allow it to be filled with the presence of the One who can.

For those of us already connected to our Creator, that connection is shaken and we examine the reality of a God who was *not* there. At least He did not show up to prevent the author of death from invading our world. We know He could have, but He did not. God can stand scrutiny, and our faith can be different, stronger, and more bold not in spite of our loss, but because of it.

Will this resource answer all your questions? Definitely not. Will you find comfort for every pain? Not all, but for some.

Will we both be richer for joining each other on this journey? I believe so.

Section One

---•◦◦◦•---

A W**IDOW**'S

VULNERABILITIES

Chapter One

Our STRONGEST EMOTIONS:
Grief and Its
Silent Partner, Depression

"Tears are often the telescope by which men see far into heaven."
—H. W. BEECHER

Have you discovered, as I have, that our emotions upon becoming a widow have an intensity we never experienced before? Grief, loneliness, anger, disappointment—these are not new emotions to us. What took me by surprise was the power, the all-consuming grip, the sudden shock of an emotion rolling over me, literally rendering me unable to function for a moment or sometimes longer. As I searched for help, I discovered many books on grief, some helpful, some not. There were fewer resources on other emotions that were specifically relevant to widows. While these emotions are similar for people who experience other losses, somehow ours is different.

While offering insights and resources on several emotions, I do recognize that these emotions—loneliness, anger, grief, depression—cannot be neatly sorted out, each in its separate compartment. At times they clump together like an army intent on taking us out. At other times we experience one "solo." We know some facts about our emotions as widows. It's comforting to know that, while we don't like the feelings, they are common, to be expected, and indeed normal, considering our loss.

Facts we know about emotions:

- ◆ Our emotions are intense. Why? Two became one and now half of us is ripped away. Every aspect of our life changes, like it or not, ready or not.
- ◆ Our emotions must be acknowledged. Denial is not a healthy permanent option. Admitting what we feel is the beginning of moving forward and being able to make changes in our new life.
- ◆ Our emotions can become empowering and energizing and a positive force as we create a new life. I realize this may be hard to believe if you are in those early months or even years.

So, my dear sister, let's start by looking at grief. From the many widows whose stories I have heard, this is the *first* emotion they face. While loneliness, anxiety, and fear toss us like a splash on the ocean, grief becomes an enveloping storm with wind and waves battering over us. Surprisingly, my lifelines came from other widows who had started the journey before me. Rich with compassion, wise from experience, strong in their resolve, they assured me my grief was normal. We all grieve so differently. I was given permission to be real, which is empowering and the key to survival for us all.

Read on. I trust you will find comfort and healing here.

GRIEF

In spite of the countless books written on grief, I've found it to be the least understood emotion we experience upon losing our dearest companion. My grieving started early as I knew my husband's illness had no cure and would progress to his anticipated death. Being a reader and researcher, I looked for help early. "Anticipatory grief," I discovered was the label for this wave that was sweeping over me while Bob was still here. Even as I audibly heard him tell me he loved me, I felt the ache of grieving inside knowing I would not hear those words much longer. How could I experience such joy at the words of his tender, baritone voice and feel such pain inside at the same time?

I don't know that discovering a label for my feelings helped, but at least I knew I was not crazy, just grieving early.

If I could find one word to describe why our grief is different from others with loss, it would be this:

FINAL

FINAL   FINAL   FINAL

Over. No second chance, no future hope, no rewind or replay.

A divorcée may daydream about a reunion. Many hope for some resolution of issues either small or large. A sense of closure or even future friendship with the former spouse might be ahead. Not for the widow.

Having a career go sour, getting fired, or retiring are events that cause people grief. The dashed career could yet morph into something different and productive. The one fired can fantasize that the boss will call back. The retiree is free though days may feel empty. The widow's loss to death is absolutely final. I am not saying our grief is greater than others; simply that it is different.

Much has been written about the stages of grief. The phases in general include initial shock followed by disbelief, then anger, which may move into depression. Finally, on our own timetable, we move into acceptance. What many of us have discovered is that we don't move through the stages in any predictable manner. The grieving process refuses to fit into neat packages. Grief defies the outline. Having talked with many widows, I've learned that we can move forward and then discover ourselves back in disbelief again.

Since that is our reality, I will not talk about stages but rather our experiences in grief. Please know, too, that this is collective wisdom. I am privileged to have women in my new circle of friends who have been on this journey much longer than I. Watching the richness of their lives, I gladly share the insights they have passed on to me.

NO COMPARISON, PLEASE!

Your grief is unique. When we cry, where we cry, what prompts our pain is so, so personal. Please do not compare yourself with another person. We are frequently asked, "How are you doing?" When you are asked that question do you find your mind leaping to another widow? *Am I recovering as fast as she is? If not, what's wrong with me?*

My dear friend, does anyone know *all* that you are grieving now? Yes, people realize you lost your husband. But do they know that you are also suffering from the loss of future dreams? Do they know the plans you had that will never materialize? Do they know that the 75 percent departure [2] of your friendship network hurts too? We'll talk about this at length in chapter 6. Losing our friends in addition to losing our mate results in one shock after another.

If you are a parent, you think of the advice your husband will never offer your children as they go through life's big passages. You think of marriages, career choices, grandchildren's events. You will face these life events alone. Please allow yourself to grieve in whatever way and for any amount of time that this emotion floats through your soul.

Grief is a messy emotion. Its face can be tearstained, blank, or a pasted-on smile. Sometimes we camouflage it well. Other times there is no mask stiff enough and large enough to cover the fact that we are engulfed in the moment. How do we get through it? Of the following thoughts, I hope at least some will be helpful.

MOVING THROUGH GRIEF

Be kind to yourself. Sleep in if you need to. You are the one who knows best how to take care of yourself. Curl up in your fuzzy robe and slippers and sip tea. Stop to watch the turtledoves. Take a deep breath. Wander slowly through a park.

Give yourself permission to forget the task at hand. Grieving takes time and work. If we don't allow ourselves to stop and recall, stop and weep, stop and drink in a memory, we miss a valuable moment of healing and of moving forward. Many of us have jobs, and we need to negotiate going back to work after our husband's death. Some of us have no choice; others can choose a return time. My contract allowed five working days to grieve for an immediate family member. I'm thankful that a doctor's recommendation gave me a few more days. Some rush back to work for the security of a familiar schedule in their topsy-turvy world.

Write in a journal. If this has already been one of your habits, you may find the volume of what you record increases. My journal became a way I still spoke to Bob. I still wrote my reflections to God, but it became important for me to let Bob know "all that was going on." If you and your husband conversed much, you understand. For those not on this journey, they may not understand that sometimes we talk to our dear mate. I found myself doing this especially while driving. Did other drivers think that this solo woman who was mouthing an animated conversation with no one crazy? My mental response: *Who cares?* If they had known Bob, they'd want to talk to him too!

> *Surround yourself
> with positive people.
> You know who they are.*

Surround yourself with positive people. You know who they are. If you have been a helper and encourager to others in the past, it may be hard for you to *not* make yourself available to those who would drain you at this time. Some people actually seek out those who are grieving. They want to connect to tell them of *their* losses and woes. Maybe later, maybe not at all. But not now. Please know that your emotional tank is already low, and you cannot risk it being drained further by their stories. While grief support groups help some, they are not for everyone. When the program includes going over each person's story, this may be too much for you in the early weeks. For some, the new group of people who understand are their lifeline. Again, you choose.

Be wary of people who want to direct your life. Yes, we are

vulnerable, especially at this time. We have needs. But giving control of our life to another, even temporarily, puts moving forward on hold. We will likely move backward and find it painful to extract ourselves from that relationship in order to begin building our own life.

Give yourself permission to try new things. Visit a place that has no memories. Change your schedule—mealtime, sleep time— discover a comfortable new routine. Eat foods you've never tried before. Look for something on television that is new, curious, interesting, or funny. (I can no longer watch *Cash Cab*, which Bob enjoyed, but *This House Is Worth What?* is intriguing, especially the international version.) Change the daily newspaper you take. I'm now reading the London-based *Financial Times* as my daily news and finding it gives a refreshing worldview compared to its New York–based counterpart.

When it feels right, change the furniture layout in a room.

Follow your own wish on when, how, and whether to dispose of your husband's things. I read a checklist that advised giving away clothing at least by the third month following your loss. (The reason given was that they would soon be out of style and not as useable to others.) Egads! Please! More than one year after my loss, I am still comforted by Bob's closet. However, I know of a person who had to move within two months due to an unmanageable mortgage, so she did not have the luxury of keeping things. We all must do what we must do—without laying guilt on someone else or expecting others to do as we do.

Grief weakens the immune system, so attend to your health. This is a tough one. If you became a widow suddenly, unexpectedly, you may be feeling apathetic about yourself. So much simply does not matter anymore. Maybe you, like me, spent months and years being your mate's primary caregiver. You are tired. I understand. Your weight has changed; you can't remember the last time you called a doctor for *yourself*. I stayed in that "Who cares?" space for several months. Perhaps we are numbed by grief or have no reserve to focus on ourselves as we simply make it through each hour, each day. But I assure you that it feels good when you are able to focus on some exercise that renews your body and your mind. I chose not to return to running, a decision my knees are grateful for. I stopped when Bob was diagnosed with amyotrophic lateral sclerosis. It seemed cruel for me to step out our door in running shoes given the diagnosis he had to face. But now I'm lap swimming regularly, something that Bob and I did not do together, and I love it. It's healing to body and mind.

No two life journeys are identical.

It bears repeating that comparing yourself to others is not productive. First, the reasons we grieve are so different. Many are private. Second, we are created so differently as individuals, including the intensity of our emotions. Finally, no two life journeys are identical. Each widow's circumstances will dictate the attention she can devote to moving through grief. My friend Mary found it in her best interests to increase her hours at the hospital to sometimes sixty per week after Brandt's exit to heaven. Some of us as friends were concerned, but we trusted her wisdom. More than thirteen months later, she retired and moved to another state. Along with the move came a new wave of grieving as intense as when her Brandt went to heaven. But her progress through grief was unique to her, and best for her, as was her plan for dealing with it.

So why do we tend to compare one's way of grieving with another's? There's no good reason. Our personalities, health, circumstances, and support systems are unique. Rather than judge, let's grant freedom. Rather than analyze, let's accept. Rather than compare, let's show compassion.

WHAT THE BIBLE SAYS ABOUT GRIEF

The Bible is not silent on the subject of grief; indeed, you'll find many passages of sadness and lament. But here are just two:

First Thessalonians 4:13: *But we do not want you to be uninformed, brothers and sisters, about those who have died, so that you may not grieve as others do who have no hope* (NRSV).

We grieve, but when we know heaven is our future there is hope beyond our tears. A phrase I say often these days is, "Heaven is looking better every day."

Psalm 56:8: *You have kept record of my days of wandering. You have stored my tears in your bottle and counted each of them* (ᴄᴇᴠ).

God would not collect our tears in a bottle if our grieving were not precious moments with Him.

DEPRESSION

Grief has a silent partner: depression. While they are not universally always partners, for us grief usually arrives first, followed by depression. The statistics on depression and widows are, indeed, depressing. However, as you read this, remember that we are not defined by numbers!

One-third of women upon becoming widows meet the criteria for clinical depression within two months.[3] One year later half of those are still clinically depressed. While some people may be surprised by this, I think it is to be expected, considering the magnitude of this event and the nature of depression.

First, may I offer you a definition of depression that may be new to you?

*Depression is a **normal** reaction*
to loss, crisis, or any traumatic event.

Psychologists and medical doctors generally agree on observable symptoms. They speak of clinical depression (i.e., when the normal reaction to loss, crisis, or any traumatic event intensifies and the symptoms interfere with normal, productive living), which typically includes:

1. moodiness (or sadness)
2. painful thinking (negative thoughts about self, lack of motivation, indecision)
3. physical symptoms of sleeplessness and loss of appetite

4. anxiety resulting in irritability
5. delusional thinking

Of these five symptoms it seems to me that most are normal, to be expected, and quite appropriate given the immensity of our loss! So here's some good news about depression:

It's normal. (We are not crazy!)
It's manageable. (We will move through it.)
It's treatable. (For some, medical and/or therapeutic assistance is needed and helpful.)

What causes it?

The traumatic event that triggers depression for us is, obviously, the loss of our husband. Our friends and acquaintances know and acknowledge that. What they do not see or know, and what sometimes even takes us by surprise, are the myriad of other losses that accompany no longer having our husband in our life. As we said earlier, our circle of friends, our routine, our social life, and the size of our income change. Our address may change since moving is sometimes necessary or beneficial. Our travel plans, our shared goals, our dreams no longer exist in the same way they used to. The list grows the more we ponder it. In order *not* to experience the symptoms of depression, we would have to be robots!

I have a new friend in her second year of widowhood. She is vivacious, energetic, and to outside appearances parenting her five children splendidly. However, it's hard! Sometimes in her secret moments she says, "Okay, David, it's time for you to show up now. This is too much!"

Would anyone blame her for momentarily thinking, "His plane is just late" or "This has just been an overlong meeting." For those of us who have caught ourselves watching the driveway at 6:15 p.m., we understand. Delusional? No, not given our loss—this is normal.

WHY IS EACH WIDOW'S REACTION UNIQUE?

There is a growing body of research on depression in widows. Given my graduate degree in counseling, I hoped to discover great, helpful nuggets there. As I read the information, I found that much of the research findings are common sense. Research shows that the incidence and extent of depression depends on the length of our marriage and the quality of that relationship. (Of course!) Women who had had longer, satisfying marriages were more likely to experience depression than those who had been married for fewer years and/or whose marital relationship was not as intimate a bond at best, or troubled and dysfunctional at worst. (Naturally.) I have known women who were contemplating divorce when their husbands became terminally ill. Yes, their recovery from widow-hood understandably appeared faster. They were already prepared to give up what they lost.

Research shows that the extent of depression depends in part on a person's physical and mental health at the time of her loss, as well as her network of friends.

We don't move into the trauma of our loss with a blank life slate. Women who have struggled with depression prior to this crisis often are back in the struggle. How did we face crises in our past? Most of us, by this time, have had other traumas to face: post-partum depression, an unexpected, unwanted move, heartbreak over a child's choices, divorce, or the death of others we cared for deeply. How did we move forward?

Healthy recovery *always requires* that we change. When a major life change comes—crisis, trauma, or whatever—we *must* either change to accommodate the new reality or hurt forever.

Those tools we used in the past to move forward positively, given our loss, can be summoned again to help us today. The extent of depression can be affected by using successful tools from our past and developing new ones.

So how do we move through depression? I hope of the following ideas, at least a few will be helpful if depression is your struggle.

Accept the fact that events in real living may result in depression. We are not guaranteed a trauma-free life, and we've been hit by one of the biggest upheavals we'll ever face. Therefore, depression is normal, and there's no need to feel guilty about being normal. Feeling guilty that you are depressed serves no positive purpose. In my observation, Christians are especially good at feeling guilty about being depressed! Give it up, sister!

When depression waves its flag, pay attention. The symptoms of clinical depression should be addressed. You may be able to address them on your own. If not, seek counsel and/or medical intervention. Many widows find that an antidepressant is helpful for a short period of time when their emotions are interfering with daily living.

Remember what the professionals can and cannot do:
They can

- Help you identify sources of your problems
- Help you clarify and see additional choices you can make
- Validate straight thinking
- Prescribe medication when appropriate

They cannot

- Change your circumstances
- Change or fix your past
- Create your future
- Change you

Make adjustments. For example, to remain stuck over worries about reduced income does not fix the problem. I have included a chapter on finances in this book. In addition, there are good books, articles, and Internet information to help you manage the resources you have. We learn, we change, we budget. We can learn to be content with what we have. And grieving our lost friendships does not need to lead to depression. We forgive, let go, and enjoy our smaller social network and a few close friends.

I am not surprised that half of the widows who experience depression are still depressed a year after their loss. Change takes time. No one else can dictate your schedule. There are so many necessary changes. If the adjustment were as easy as cleaning out the refrigerator, we'd all be dancing within a few months.

Small steps are better than no steps.

Address health issues. You'll find this tip for each emotion. Depression seems to be especially connected to other health issues. The hospitalization rate for the recently bereaved is 600 times that of other people.[4] Facing surgery alone, delayed recovery time due to grief, discombobulated living patterns can all intensify depression. If your "who cares?" attitude is preventing you from addressing a health issue, enlist a friend as your support system or accountability partner. Encourage each other with weight goals or daily walking. Small steps are better than no steps. Celebrate and enjoy each accomplishment. God values our bodies. They are important enough to Him that each is an original. We only get one. We can replace some parts, but not the whole thing—in this life.

A BIBLICAL PERSPECTIVE ON DEPRESSION

First Kings 19 describes behavior by Elijah that meets the criteria for clinical depression. God attended to his physical needs and gave him a new purpose in life. God did not ignore or condemn Elijah's feelings, and He does not ignore or condemn ours. He moves with us and in us, through them. God continued to use Elijah after his season of despair.

Read Lamentations 3:19–25. Depression need not consume us. You'll see that God is always compassionate and gives us a new morning. The new morning is not just the sun rising the next day— it is the new and fresh opportunity that comes with change.

Yes, we may fall in the crisis, as Psalm 145:14–19 acknowledges, but we do not stay down. Our Lord takes our hand when we are down and lifts us up.

We see that it is God's habit to be real with His people where they are. Thank God for that! We really don't need platitudes or superficial stuff on our journey through grief or depression.

He walks with us on our journey whether we sense His presence or not. Psalm 118:6 tells us that "The Lord is with me; I will not be afraid. What can man do to me?"

He offers us a new day in which the necessity of making different choices becomes the opportunity to change. Psalm 118:24 encourages us to remember that "This is the day the Lord has made; let us rejoice and be glad in it."

He lifts our chin, takes our hand, and guides our steps. We are not alone.

Chapter Two

$\mathcal{F}$EAR:

Normal in Change,
but Temporary

———⊶⊷———

"The surf that distresses the ordinary swimmer produces
in the surf-rider the super joy of going straight through it."
—OSWALD CHAMBERS

$\mathcal{D}$oes fear have a new face in your life as a widow? Do the night
sounds in your home seem different from the ones you heard
before you were alone? When you turn on the ignition, does your
car whine at you in a way it did not whine at your husband? And
what about this insurance bill? Was it always so large? I walked
alone to the Metra train station after dark. Peering down through
the bridge's grates into the Chicago River, I actually thought the
water was darker because Bob was not at my side.

In my early months of being alone, I was frequently drawn to
Bob's resting place. I'd speed down the Illinois tollway with my
mind visualizing the gentle beauty of the Bruce Lake Cemetery. I
made the six-hour road trip so many times that I often drove on
autopilot as my mind rehearsed all I wanted to tell him. One time
I realized I had missed the exit I needed. The Indiana exit appeared
suddenly on the right, and I was in the far left lane. How had it
come up so fast? I *had* to exit. Driving sixty miles per hour with a
chain of speeding semis between me and where I must go, I had
few choices. I braked and pulled onto the left shoulder, shaking. In

moments like these during my first year as a widow, the large, enveloping, sometimes suffocating emotion of grief was instantly vaporized by fear. This fear could take control so completely that it could make me perspire profusely (in other words, sweat buckets) on a cold night. It was fear that prevented me from realizing that if I missed an exit, I could always get off the expressway at the next opportunity. It could wipe from my brain the reality that if something happened while driving, I have a roadside service to call for help and I have a financial plan as a resource.

Fear has the power to do all that and more. Fear can cause us to decide when, where, and whether we go places. Fear can make us think it's equally out of the question to visit a friend nearby or in a faraway country. Fear can cause us to doubt our ability to take control of our life. Fear can convince us our future is small. In fact, fear can even convince us we are crazy.

So if the question is, "Shall we master this emotion?" I would say, "We must!"

As we mentioned earlier, facing an emotion after we become a widow brings with it our experiences from the past. If you had been bold as an adolescent, and carried this courageous spirit into your adult years, pushing the boundaries of your world with little fear, this emotion will likely not be debilitating to you. Fear will come, but you will summon whatever resources you used before to prevent fear from shrinking your world.

For more timid women, overcoming fear may be a greater challenge. When there were challenging situations in the past, did you ask someone else to fix the problem? Did you count on someone else to sort out the paperwork, to drive, to confront, to solve?

Our past habits need not, and should not, dictate our future. But we gain insight into our own behavior by asking, "How did I get to this place?"

There is no shame or harm in acknowledging that we may not have been the primary family driver or navigator. Walking solo at some times and in some places may have been a rare event. We may not have been the overseer of vehicles or budgets. But we are now.

You will repeatedly hear me state that becoming a widow is a new opportunity for change. We know everything *has* changed. We can choose the direction, and whether it is positive or negative.

YOU HAVE A BOARD OF DIRECTORS

May I introduce you to a concept that is helping me navigate change? I introduce it here because this concept is particularly helpful in addressing fear. It also is helpful with the myriad of decisions we have to make.

Imagine a boardroom with a large impressive table. High-back chairs surround it. You sit at the head of the table. Each chair represents a person to advise you, to vote on your actions, and bring you information. You listen to these people whether you wish to or not. They are your VIPs, the movers and shakers of your world, the POIs (people of influence) in your life.

What determines who sits in each chair? Likely, two were, and perhaps are, your parents. You invite favorite teachers or relatives to join your board. Life events may result in an intruder. If your parents divorced, one parent may vacate their chair and someone not of your choosing sits down. Their power over your life may give them VIP status whether you like it or not.

Take a pad of paper and sketch your table and chairs. Imagine your board of directors. Who are they? Label each chair. We typically have a board of directors in our youth that is determined by our family, culture, and circumstances. Individual board members change as we move through the stages of our lives. At one time you may have six chairs and in another season fifteen. Not all are of equal importance, but each matters to you.

> *Directors may be as diverse as a person who lived in a previous century, or it may be your twin sister.*

Some of us welcome to our table people we have never met. In the graduate school season of my life, I devoured the writings of Francis and Edith Schaeffer. As a believer, marriage partner, and mother, I invited Edith to my table. I "listened" to her through her books on faith, family, and hospitality. Because of her presence at my table, Neff hospitality happened in a new and different way.

Directors may be as diverse as a person who lived in a previous century, or it may be your twin sister. You may not even recognize the importance of these people until you do this exercise!

With each major life event, someone changes on your board.

A new career may bring a new mentor you trust and value. A geographical move combined with a busy schedule may eventually remove a director. They just fade away. Given the reality that we are all human—subject to messing up in small and large ways—some of our VIPs misstep, disappoint us, show themselves unfit to sit at our table. The commercial that says "life comes at us fast" is an understatement. Our changing board of directors reflects that.

And now you are a widow. Your husband was a VIP. If he was good and wise, his input in your life was huge and positive. Even if he was unwise like the biblical character Nabal, he still was a POI. He will likely continue to be one of your VIPs for months and years to come. You will need to put aside the messages he left in your mind.

Some of your directors may disappear. In chapter 6 we'll talk about our shrinking friendship network. We may be surprised by those who removed themselves from our lives. Some even had board status. Yes, their departure hurt. But life is real; behavior does not lie; and life must go on. That empty chair is a positive opportunity for another valuable individual who cares about you with your current circumstance and status as a widow.

So why go to such lengths to examine who sits at your board? Because you are now facing a great opportunity to choose. With the myriad of choices you must now make, this is a good time to evaluate who belongs at your table. And in your new circumstance some should be invited to exit.

A word of caution: Some of us have discovered that upon our loss, some pull their chair up to our table uninvited. I have seen adult children make this move (thankfully not in my boardroom). This is not unique to widows. Divorcées tell me they experience similar strategic moves and attempted takeovers at their tables.

This is a key time to take advantage of our changing world. We can evaluate and select a wise board for the challenges we face.

CHOOSING YOUR BOARD OF DIRECTORS

May I suggest six people you need at your table? You may have many more. These are actually positions with a function that need to be fulfilled in your new life. The list is in no particular order, and some individuals may even fill two positions. I suggest these people: a godly widow, a person with financial wisdom, a practical friend, an encourager, a person with spiritual discernment and courage, and a relative whose priority is *your* well-being.

1. A godly widow

Before I became a widow, I would never have imagined the value of another widow in my life. Would not any wise person who has experienced loss be helpful?

Yes. But not enough.

There is a difference between a widow and those who have experienced other losses. We have said before that the marriage bond is unique—think of the way married people sometimes come to look like each other and develop similar mannerisms, for instance—and defies description in many ways. It's so 24/7. Only another widow can relate to that.

When I began a Bible study for widows at my church, we experienced a new and unique bond for a group of mostly strangers. When we shared our stories in our small groups, eyes met with more than sympathy and empathy; compassionate understanding met us where we were.

While I have been privileged to have several godly widows in my life now, let me tell you of one who sits in my boardroom.

I dialed Paula's phone number in the fall of 2003. I had known of her and her husband, Tom, years earlier through a church we attended. My husband had fallen that summer and tests "could not rule out amyotrophic lateral sclerosis." Paula's husband died in July of 2003 of this deadly disease, and mutual friends believed she might be helpful in my days of confusion and distress. She agreed to meet me on my lunch break at a restaurant near the high school where I counseled. I did not know what to expect. I see now my audacity in asking her for help only a few months after her loss.

Walking up to the restaurant, I was met by a beautiful woman who exuded peace. She had that compassionate understanding in her eyes. She knew my future in ways I could not have known, nor would I have wanted to know, at that time.

As we got acquainted, our salads were neglected and our common bonds explored. I discovered a woman with an open heart, an open soul toward God's hand in her life, and a willingness to answer any question I asked.

Hurrying back to school, students, and the relentless schedule were minor challenges compared to going home that night and seeing my husband, knowing more of his journey and our future. However, *I was no longer in it alone.*

As my journey with Bob and his disease stretched from months into years, I could and did call Paula at any time, with any problem, or just to be heard and understood as no one else could. Realizing now the grief and woundedness of her own soul, I cannot fathom how she could give so much, and how she was able to comfort me so wisely with her own loss so fresh.

Because of her example, I am now in contact with another woman on the same journey we've been on.

But there's more. After Bob's graduation to heaven, I knew from God's direction that having a widows' Bible study in our church would be a good thing. The first person I called to join me in the trenches of leadership in this new adventure was Paula. She was available once again, and I have been helped by her counsel in this new arena. She courageously tells me when she sees my "wishful thinking" affect my behavior. She sees my weakness when I think I am strong. She discerns when, in my bold desire to move forward, I try to suppress some of my own pain that must instead be acknowledged. She "tells it like it is" with gentle boldness. And I listen because I know she has my back.

In addition to comfort and connection, a godly widow is an

important *protection* in our vulnerability and loneliness.

After starting Widowconnection.com, I was contacted by many widows. Some offered encouragement and appreciation that this new ministry exists. Others asked for advice with problems or just wanted to share their story with someone who understood.

One widow of only a few months contacted me to say she wanted to meet someone and start dating. She wanted to know what I thought. Some people in a widows' network might encourage that, especially those without spiritual resources. I e-mailed her and advised that she not do so at this time due to her vulnerability with such a recent loss. However, I could also say to her, "I understand lonely. I understand the overlarge, empty bed. I understand the too-quiet room. I understand feeling you are in a solitary bubble in a crowded, noisy mall. Yes, I understand lonely." And then I could talk about spiritual resources for our lonely times.

If you do not have such a person in your life, the search is worth it. I would also say for this individual—as well as all others you invite to your boardroom—that listening to her words before inviting her to your table is not enough. Watch her walk. Let her behavior speak. Then decide whether one chair is hers.

2. A person with financial wisdom

While this person is quite important in your boardroom, I'll not include here a lengthy discussion of this vital aspect of your new life, since chapter 3 will be devoted to finances. We'll address there the unique challenges widows face related to money, and lay out practical steps for getting our finances in order.

For our purposes here, however, we do need to have an informed voice at our table who "gets it" when it comes to managing resources God has given us for our provision. Why do we need this person? Often in marriage, women do not manage and make all the decisions about money. Some women enter widowhood knowing *nothing* about their finances. We are required to be on a quick learning curve and need information for the immediate, as well as long-term. While there are many books, articles, and Web sites that are helpful, it is wise to have an individual whose counsel we can seek. In chapter 3, we'll explore the options of professional financial advisors and how to select one. You may use those guidelines in deciding who gets a seat at your table. However, every widow's circle of acquaintances is different. You may have a wise person in your network who is money savvy and confidential, and who respects your spiritual perspective on resources.

I sought advice from several people. One of those individuals is now my primary resource and sits at my table.

Should you give this seat to a qualified relative? Probably not. In fact, you'll be doing both yourself and your family member a favor by not placing a relative on your board. I'm able to discuss options and decisions with some of my family members, and I value their input, but this isn't always the case in every situation. For example, I know of a widow whose adult child wanted the title of her home changed to his name. His plan was to use the paid-for home to secure a home equity loan for himself. But who would have to move if the adult child defaulted on the loan payment and foreclosure resulted? Whose wealth would be transferred? Whose future would be in jeopardy?

I call it "relative blindness." I've suffered from it myself at times, both to my own detriment, and the relative with whom I made the bad decision. My daughter Valerie, who has a unique ability to hold a mirror to my behavior, helped me see reality.

"Mom, if you're thinking about loaning money, imagine the loan in this way. Could you write that check and then light a match to it and watch that money disappear? Can you accept that ultimately that *loan* may turn out to be a *gift*? If that's okay, make the loan."

For that relative who is financially wise, has your best interests at heart, and could sit at your table, do both of you a favor and invite someone else to occupy this seat. Though you might have named that person to be the executor of your will, spare him or her the risks of misunderstandings or expectations of other relatives at this time.

Once you've determined who occupies this chair at your table, use this person! You have selected someone trustworthy and confidential. So when you need to replace a vehicle, call and get advice. Tell them the numbers. Where will the money come from? We'll cover this in more depth in chapter 3. But for now, utilize this director. Because he or she is interested in your well-being, your call does not annoy him. He wants to help you achieve your financial goals, especially stability and self-reliance.

Try to internalize these truths from Scripture:

"Honor the Lord with your wealth, with the firstfruits of all your crops" (Proverbs 3:9).

"The earth is the Lord's and all that is in it, the world, and those who live in it" (Psalm 24:1 NRSV).

3. A practical friend

You and I are capable of straight thinking. We can and will navigate all these changes. We can figure it out. But every widow I have met states that there were moments she did not believe in herself and her straight, commonsense thinking. I understand.

It is good, especially in those early months, to have someone to just be another pair of eyes, another set of listening ears. Sometimes fear or grief clouds our vision, and we do not see options available to us. We may have a good solution to a problem and just need someone to affirm that.

One couple who has remained in my friendship network provides that for me. Steve is a household handyman, as was Bob. During Bob's illness, he took vehicles for tire rotations and repaired chairs, and he and Carol trimmed bushes and trees, to name just a few ways they helped. He continues to be someone who can give practical advice. He and Carol listen and offer their perspective.

In one of my more outlandish attempts to be my own handyman without seeking his advice, I decided to paint the discolored, ugly grout in my white tile floor. Small project, right? I exited Home Depot with a two-gallon bucket of stucco paint (thick must be good), many two-inch sponge paintbrushes, a paint pan, and the confident smile of a successful handywoman.

Three rooms of white tile looked larger after my first hour on the floor. Bob had re-grouted once, so my coat of paint was level with the tile. The brown floorboard got in my way. Wiping the paint off the tile usually meant wiping some off my grout. Three hours later I was halfway through one room. Better stop. I examined my progress. And, well, it did not look so good. This was probably because it was dusk. I was sure that in daylight, my project would look better.

The first challenge in the morning was to get my aching body out of bed. I determined that the best solution to the pain was to work faster before my body refused to cooperate with my mind.

After completing one room, it was obvious things were going in a bad direction. I decided to stop. Tomorrow help was on the way. Ana, my miracle cleaning helper, might be able to fix this, I thought. She speaks little English, but we successfully communicate to get our tasks done.

When Ana stepped in my door onto my project, she began talking rapidly. I did not understand one word she said. But her look spoke volumes. If you can mix puzzlement with exasperation changing to humor, that was the look. She went right to work scrubbing with more than her usual vigor. She won. Thankfully, when she left, there was only enough evidence of my adventure for my children to look at the floor and ask, "What happened?" Thankfully they did not see it B.A. (before Ana).

On a dinner outing I told my friends Steve and Carol about my handywoman adventure. They laughed and I laughed until we cried and people were staring. Like I said about your financial director, don't hesitate to call! Believe me, I call Steve and Carol more frequently now, and I have an almost full two-gallon bucket of stucco paint for my next garage sale.

There may be many in your network, and you may tap them with different questions on different practical matters. The important thing is to seek other input. When I hear of widows who have been taken advantage of, it's usually because they made a mistake that could have been prevented had they sought counsel from a practical friend.

Take someone with you to the car dealership. Ask others who they use as painters, handymen, or for repair services on home systems. After I hastily hired an expensive contractor, my directors advised me to always get three competitive bids on any work or major purchase. You won't always take the lowest bid; you may decide to choose the most expensive bid for personal, safety, or quality reasons. But you'll learn much about "stuff" just by listening to the bidders justify their costs.

It has been said that the wise person is she who knows what she does not know. I would add that it is a wise person who is humble enough to invite another to advise her, or even challenge her with his or her perspective and insight.

> *"For the Lord will be your confidence and will keep your foot from being snared." (Proverbs 3:26)*

4. An encourager

Count yourself blessed if you have one person in your life who encourages you, believes in you, and always expects the best of you.

In 2001, Bob was the recipient of the Moody Alumnus of the Year award. By tradition, this was a surprise presentation during Founders Week at an evening service followed by a reception for family and friends at historic Moody Church in Chicago. I had the assignment of getting Bob there and to invite his family and friends to attend, but all were to be out of sight until after the presentation.

It was a special service and all went as planned. Bob was honored, and he accepted the award with his typical humility and gracious spirit.

Afterward at the reception, the presenter of the award stepped up to Bob's mother and me and quipped, "When someone gets such an honor, usually no one is more surprised than his wife and his mother!"

Mother Neff, without a second's hesitation, answered, "No, I just wonder what took you so long!"

Mother Neff was Bob's encourager from day one.

We all need that person in our life. If you have been the one who's a helper, a listener to others, the one who helps others up, you may never have developed a friendship where someone lifted you. Now you need such a person in your life. In fact, you may need to be careful to limit your contacts with those who drain your tank rather than fill it. We talked about this earlier related to our grieving. Besides limiting negative and sad input, we need to increase positive and encouraging input in our lives.

One widow may not need to be encouraged that she can master her finances, because she is already successful in doing so. But she may need encouragement in other areas, such as setting boundaries with her children.

One may need encouragement in marketing her skills to secure a new job or apply for scholarship money to return to school.

Another may just need someone to say, "You're doing a good job parenting alone." This compliment is especially meaningful if the person giving it can point to a specific in her child, their developing character, self-sufficient or polite behavior.

I have a new friend who saw my potential for serving and ministering to others shortly after I became a widow. As she told me what she saw in my future, I could not imagine living that life. Now, much of what Carol predicted is happening, and I'm delighting in the new challenges in my life.

On this new journey, I am learning about the paradoxes of God in a new, fresh way. One paradox is that new people are coming in my life whom I can encourage. When I do so, the experience "backfires" in a positive way. I am encouraged.

If you are reading this and want to encourage widows in your life, be real. We don't need a plastic smiley face—we need the real thing.

"I thought about you today."

"I spoke to the Father on your behalf today."

"I prayed for your children."

"I see you getting stronger."

Certainly as widows, we can say this and more to each other. If you need more ideas, examine Philippians 4:8–9. I'm discovering there is such strength in community, in moving forward together. And nothing propels us forward with more strength than encouragement.

"Finally, sisters, whatever is true, whatever is noble, whatever is right, whatever is pure, whatever is lovely, whatever is admirable— if anything is excellent or praiseworthy—think about such things. Whatever you have learned or received or heard from me, or seen in me—put it into practice. And the God of peace will be with you" (Philippians 4:8–9).

5. A person with spiritual discernment and courage

Having a spiritual mentor is a gift, a rare one, I believe. Successful businesspeople usually have a mentor to help navigate and even create their mobile path upward. Athletes have coaches. Chefs learn under master chefs. Pastors are usually paired with spiritual leaders. Personal trainers are a popular addition to people seeking healthy lifestyles.

So why wouldn't each of us who desires a growing spiritual life seek out our own trainer, coach, or mentor?

As you consider who fulfills this function in your life, remember, in order to occupy a chair at the table for your board of directors, this person needs to have some level of understanding of *you*. You need to be able to glean from him or her information relevant to *your* life.

Some of this function might be filled by a pastor. But increasingly with the megachurch movement, pastors not only do not know most of their flock, a member cannot access them. The pastor of a large church, for practical reasons, is only available to a circle of his choosing. His teachings may well provide you with some insights and guidance, but a true spiritual mentor is a person who can give input on *your* personal dilemmas, crises, relationships, having some knowledge of *your* circumstance and history.

The typical large church answer to this need is the small group. You are blessed if you are in one in which the members are mature believers and who function at an authentic level. Some groups are casual or superficial or mostly social. While that may meet some of your needs, most widows need more, especially in the first years of being alone. This need is why I believe congregations should have a ministry specifically for widows. In appendix C, I have included a church model for church leaders who want to start one. I also have included suggestions for the widow who wants to start such a group in appendix B.

Meanwhile, most of us can identify a few people in our remaining circle who have spiritual maturity and can understand our new life with its demands. If we have even one such person, she can be our lifeline. Research states that the widow who has such a network with the spiritual dimension is less likely to experience depression and lives with greater satisfaction.

For the widow who simply does not have, and cannot find, such a person, fortunately, there are books. Find those authors who comfort your soul and who write about the problems you face. You can gain knowledge from secular resources, but only wisdom from spiritual resources.

"*As iron sharpens iron, so one woman sharpens another.*" (Proverbs 27:17)

6. A relative whose priority is your well-being

I have learned from my ministry that widows' living circumstances come in all shapes and sizes, and ages and families. They have a variety of expectations from their culture and baggage— both heavy and heartening—from their marriage. Rarely is a widow totally alone. The family tree certainly changes when our husband dies, and we must adjust to that reality. We'll elaborate on families in chapter 7.

If you are the kind of people person who gravitates to reading the advice columns in magazines and newspapers (I'm one of those), you know that many advice seekers are at least puzzled, if not provoked, by the behavior of a relative. We married more than a man. We married a branch, and in that union, grafted into our tree were branches occupied by strange and wonderful birds. And while we're being real here, let's admit, some relatives are south of strange.

I'll let you glimpse into my tree by sharing a sister story. When Bob married me, he became an intimate outsider to the sisterhood composed of me and three very different sisters.

I write the following illustration with permission. My younger sister, upon becoming single again, brought two ferrets into her household for companionship. They were appropriately trained to use newspapers in the bathroom. Since her grown children visited often and there was just one bathroom, the animals would wait patiently for the door to open, enter and take their turn, and then exit. My own children were amused at this quite humanlike behavior.

"It's simple," Ardys stated. "They think they *are* humans."

Indeed, they sat on the couch and looked attentively at you as you spoke. No wonder. She talked to them as if they *were* human. (This caught my children's attention as well.)

She now lives in a home with a badly behaved tree growing exceedingly close to her home and her driveway. In a severe storm, this tree managed to deploy large branches to damage her roof and destroy her car as well. Since she did not have money to pay for removal of the remaining large tree, she "branded" the trunk by carving a face on it. When she trims various plants and shrubs, she attaches a beard of trimmings to the face. The neighbors enjoy the tree with the changing face. And Ardys? She is being herself, the epitome of creativity in the sisterhood.

Why tell such a story when you are trying to identify a relative to sit at your board? Because there is value in retaining connections to family history during this time. Your history, his history. These people have influenced you, perhaps more than you know or intended. They are not on your board to advise you on ferrets and trees. You need connection. Before you say, "No way, none of my relatives belong there," consider the richness and diversity they bring to your life.

Upon the loss of your husband, a large branch disappeared. The family tree shook. Connections were broken: your tree has a new shape. Ideally people have been grafted into a new place, and breaks and wounds will be mended over time.

I have observed that some families don't do the hard work to establish this revised tree. I have observed two major reasons for this. One is PAIN—present in capital letters when family groups assemble again. Widows have written to me with incredible stories of relatives' comments and behavior after their loss. We are supersensitive and tender as well. It's harder for us to let "stuff" slide as we might have before.

The second is money. The widow who had no shared assets and no money may, at least, be fortunate to not have money issues with relatives. (Of course, *poor* has its own issues.) Small or large sums can be the focus of disagreements and even lawsuits. It is a rare family that does not have some times of pain and hurt that threaten the health of the remaining tree.

> "*A* man of many companions
> may come to ruin, but there
> is a friend who sticks closer than
> a brother." (Proverbs 18:24)

Often we expect more from relatives after our loss than they can give, or ever could before. We want relatives to know and deliver what we need. Rarely does that happen. By identifying a levelheaded person in the tree who, with some objectivity sees them and knows them, and knows us as well, this director can help us have realistic expectations in our season of grieving and afterward. It's not unusual for major upheavals and arguments to occur related to the death of our husband. This relative on our board can help prevent smoking bridges from burning.

So now we have our board of directors.

Sometimes they weigh in on our decisions uninvited. We just know what they would say. They spot-check our behavior. Take advantage of these people. Call, e-mail, ask, probe. This lifeline can bring you satisfaction, comfort, wisdom, and protection.

Why include this concept in the chapter on fear? Because these directors can be our first line of defense when fear threatens to restrict the well-being and moving forward of our lives. Talk to them specifically about the new fears in your life. Listen to their perspective. They may have advice and/or ideas to keep your life large. After all, fear can keep us from traveling, driving to new places, meeting new people, and much more. Given our loss, we do not need or wish for our world to shrink even more.

After talking with another couple, one in which the husband travels extensively and my friend is alone much of the time, I opted to get rid of older vehicles for a quite dependable, safe vehicle. Purchasing a GPS (global positioning system) is a wise investment for many of us who are on the road a lot. Some widows install security systems in their homes. With each decision we make that addresses our fears, we feel ourselves growing more confident. As our competence as a single person grows, we need our board of directors less. But we are still thankful they are in our lives and available when we need them.

A BIBLICAL PERSPECTIVE ON FEAR

Scripture is clear that reverential fear of our Creator is necessary and appropriate. I see no other fear in Scripture that dictates believers' behavior. Here are some examples.

Mary and Joseph escaped to Egypt with their infant son, Jesus. Caesar had issued the edict to kill all infant boys under the age of two. They fled based on obedience, because God told them to go. Might their human emotions have felt fear on the journey? Probably so; see Matthew 2:13–14.

Paul went to Jerusalem despite the likelihood of his arrest there. His calling to teach there trumped fear for his survival (Acts 20).

Esther approached King Ahasuerus uninvited, an action that was against the law. Rather than fear the consequences of this action, she simply stated, "If I perish, I perish" (Esther 4:16).

Abigail struck out on a donkey directing a food caravan as a gift to her husband, Nabal's, avowed enemy, David. On that ride through the heat and treacherous pathway, did she fear David's rejection of her gift? Did she fear returning home to her foolish, hotheaded (some scholars surmise he was an alcoholic based on verses 17 and 36) husband? Possibly. But neither fear stopped her (1 Samuel 25).

In this spirit and following these biblical examples, my encouragement to you and me, as well, is that we not allow fear to stop us. To work, travel, serve, encourage, visit, vacation—all of these are things we can do, and places we can go.

Does that mean we ignore and deny the fears we feel? Not at all. If you'd like a rich study in Scripture, study the 326 references to fear. "Fear not" appears eighty times. List your fears. Which of these Scriptures apply to you specifically? There is an unexplainable power to overcome fear by knowing Scripture. We recognize that our lives are in the hands of One who has greater power than any frightening force in our lives.

I have shared one of my stories of facing fear in *Christianity Today* (January 2008). I'll include it here for humor and your encouragement.

A moment of great change in my life occurred in the Dominican Republic. I was treasuring a week of rest and relaxation after four of the hardest years of my life. Three years of caring for Bob in his illness, retiring from my career, and wading through the depths of those first months alone had taken a large toll on my body and soul. This was my first trip alone. While I had expected to rest and read, this place had other options. I found myself signing up for any and all activities: snorkeling, horseback riding, and learning to sail a catamaran.

First I took out a kayak. The ocean was smooth in the morning and the beaches were awesome to explore. Next I took a motorboat ride to a different area for snorkeling. I followed a brilliant school of blue fish for a delicious distance and then lifted my head to see where our small boat was. Not in sight. Now that was an unnerving moment. A gentle swell lifted me. There it was: the boat had not left without me. I was back to following the beauty below.

And how can I describe horseback riding again? My horse loved to run. Did she sense that I did too? Galloping along beautiful beaches was delicious. Each adventure topped the one the day before.

Next was my catamaran sailing lesson. As I was the only single woman to sign up for solo sailing lessons, my instructor eyed me with little enthusiasm. He was probably wishing to have been
assigned a couple or one of the many single males. A female and well beyond thirty-nine years of age was not his typical student. He told me where to plant myself on the canvas. My eager attitude was soon deflated. He said, "You can't learn this. I'll take you for a ride and we'll go back."

Wrong, wrong, wrong, I thought. Underestimating my physical muscle was expected. But after my life of the last four years, my mental muscle had been strengthened, and "can't" did not describe me!

On my fourth lesson my new instructor (I had requested change in instructors) said these delightful words: "You can dump me now." I wanted to smile a large idiotic grin. I coolly returned us to the beach, dumped him, and headed back out on the ocean. Facing the distant horizon, just the sail, rudder, canvas, and me, I let that largest grin spread from sunburned ear to ear.

There are no words to describe being alone on that canvas, gripping the rudder, feeling the wind at your back, and racing out into the Atlantic! "Honey, can you see me?" I shouted to the sky. It was as if he answered, "You'll do this and more, sweetheart, and I'm not surprised."

Back home after I described my adventure to my family, my grandson asked, "Nana, weren't you afraid?"

"No," was my definite answer. "If I had failed and drowned, I'd see God and Grandpa. If I succeeded, I've sailed a catamaran—solo. Nana has nothing to lose."

I can say to you, we have stared death in the face as few have, and we're still standing, my friend. Let me assure you, you can. We have nothing to fear. Let the sweet, gentle current of freedom carry you forward.

Chapter Three

YES, WE CAN!

Money

––––⊗⊗⊗⊗––––

"Patience is power; with time and patience the mulberry leaf becomes silk."
—CHINESE PROVERB

Whether clutching a worn wallet with a few small, green wrinkled bills inside, holding a checkbook with enough funds for a month, or owning a fat portfolio, most widows are concerned about money. Our surveys show that finances are consistently first or second in importance in the issues we face when our husband dies. Widows who have little money wonder, "How will I live?" Widows with much wonder, "How can I manage and protect this?"

Most widows are in the how-will-I-live? group.

Maybe your husband's attitude was, "Don't worry, honey, I've taken care of everything." (Translation: The shoe box in my closet with random papers makes sense to me.)

Or: "Our financial planner is on top of all this." (Translation: There is a good plan in place; I was uncomfortable bringing you into the discussion.)

Or complete silence. Amazingly many couples never discuss the likelihood of "till death do us part" actually happening.

"I'd like to talk to you about our finances." One widow remembers her husband inviting her to that conversation. She declined because she trusted that all was well, and she was disinterested in finance. Shortly after his death, she discovered about $100,000 of hidden debt that she was obligated to repay. How she wished they had had the talk!

Stories new widows send to my Web site about money are usually not funny, and sometimes even tragic. An all-too-common element is that of surprise.

Typically upon becoming a widow or widower, our income need is 80 percent of our need as a married couple. A widow's new income is typically 63 percent of our income as a married couple. A widower's income is typically 80 percent of his income as a married couple. This statistic explains why most widows struggle with their decline in finances.

While each circumstance is different, some guidelines apply to us all. The buck now stops with us, literally. We can become competent and self-sufficient. We often don't know that truth in our early months of being alone.

Each of us needs only three things to master our finances:

1. The desire to do so. (Necessity is a good motivator as well.)
2. The willingness to read and become informed.
3. Basic math skills of adding and subtracting, or a calculator.

Where do we start? Often our mind skips back, fearing to tackle our finances. Why didn't he tell me? Why didn't we do this together? Don't despair—it is not productive to look back. It is not unusual for couples not to have discussed the likelihood that one would leave this earth before the other. Of course, those are not pleasant conversations. Regardless of circumstances, let's start at the beginning.

Please know there is a huge reward for tackling this important part of your life. There is great peace of mind in getting a handle on your money. This peace softens the rawness of our emotions, our anxiety, our grieving. Those feelings do not go away, but peace about our financial future is a good thing.

OUR FIRST TEN STEPS

(Don't be overwhelmed with
ten steps, but think one step at a time.)

1. Don't make any major decisions for a while.
2. Start tracking all your expenses. Basic budget forms are included in appendix F.
3. Pay your bills promptly.
4. Call Social Security to obtain survivor benefits, or go to my website Widowconnection.com. Links will take you to the appropriate forms.
5. Find out how much you have in assets, and discover your liabilities as well.
6. Organize all financial documents.
7. Talk to other wise people about their choices, including appropriate VIPs on your board of directors, but make your own decisions.
8. Reinvest your money.
9. Maintain your budget.
10. Reallocate investments as needed.

1. Don't make any major decisions for a while.

Times of turmoil are typically not times of clear thinking. I hear so many stories, from sad to horrific, of women who have made their circumstances worse by acting quickly. Yes, there are some instances where an immediate decision is necessary. One widow, facing a large mortgage, two leased car payments, and credit card bills, had to put her home on the market, and secure less expensive housing in order to begin to get her financial affairs in order. Most experts advise that you not sell your residence immediately, however, if you don't absolutely have to. Wait until your life takes on its new rhythm and then make that decision.

Widows are frequently preyed on with offers of great deals on an investment. And a lump sum life insurance payment may seem like lots of money to a woman who has not managed finances before. One widow lost $200,000 of life insurance money in two years on a hot tip from her husband's "friend." Having been a stay-at-home mom, she found herself in the job market sooner than she wished to be, poorer, but wiser.

Depending on your age, especially for older widows, that life insurance check may be the biggest, or at least the centerpiece, of your income for the rest of your life. Consider these facts:

Median income of people over 65 (2005)

$21,784—median income of males over 65

$12,495—median income of females over 65

12.3% of women over 65 live in poverty.

7.3% of men over 65 live in poverty.[5]

What contributes to widows having less than widowers?

During earning years, women's income is $.80 to men's $1.00.

Men start investing in their late twenties.

Women start investing in their thirties to forties.

Women average fewer years of employment with less opportunity for building up a pension.

Combining meager retirement services, declining earning power, and lack of experience investing, the fact that is if women live to their mid-eighties, many outlive their funds.

If you have money to invest, whether from life insurance or other sources, begin to educate yourself as a businesswoman. Resist the immediate option of purchasing annuities, as they are an expensive tool that typically results in your money later going to the company selling the annuity, not to your family.

Be alert to the temptation to be an impulse buyer as a source of comfort. Yes, you are hurting, but increasing your credit card balance is counterproductive at best, and lethal to your financial future and credit score at worst. Instead, take a long walk, watch the sunset with a cup of tea, take comfort in God's creation, or create a simple scrapbook. True comfort is free.

2. *Start tracking all your expenses.*

Are you a paper-and-pencil person? Do you like computer tools? Fortunately, you have lots of user-friendly resources available. If you and your husband kept a budget together, staying with that method will simplify your life when everything seems to be in a tailspin.

If you did not keep the family books or participate in the process, never fear. YES, YOU CAN! If you are a paper-and-pencil person, we'll walk through the process together. If you wish to use the computer, you might go to the Crown Financial Ministries Web site, or see Suze Orman's Web site or her books. While Orman's information does not have a spiritual basis, it is sound and especially helpful for women. Her sense of empowerment is beneficial and important for widows.

If you are already using a computer, you may wish to purchase software such as Quicken or Microsoft Money. Excel spreadsheets can be personalized or you can create your own in Numbers on Apple. If you are a beginner, allow yourself time to learn and experiment. I would recommend beginning with a simple program (which is usually less expensive) for starters. Crown Financial Ministries offers a practical budget tool called Mvelopes for about $8.00 monthly. Their program offers online bill payments and support services that are helpful in getting started.

If budgeting is a new adventure in your life, I recommend a paper/pencil beginning. Learning computer software can even be frustrating when you are at your best and are equipped with loads of patience. This is not that moment in time. Don't get distracted or frustrated by the fact that you do not know what your consistent monthly income will be. You need not have established a basic budget yet; in fact, this first step will help you get to that point.

Just start writing everything down.

While this step requires no mathematics, no profound economic insights, not even five minutes a day, it is the single greatest step you will take toward financial freedom.

Many widows don't know where money needs to go. We may also not realize how much we are spending on "little" things.

At the end of each month, as you total each category, you will see your real financial behavior. Then you can ask yourself the questions, "Is this what I want?" "Does this reflect wise balances for my future?" "What changes can I make?" "What changes must I make?"

After a few months, complete a Monthly Income and Expenses sheet. I include one in appendix F. Again, you can download it and print from Widowconnection.com: Under Moving Forward, click on Finances; then click on Basic Budget Tools. Use your findings and decisions to establish your budget.

Congratulations!

You've started! It gets easier and—trust me—actually becomes fun!

3. *Pay your bills promptly.*

If a bill is specifically your husband's, you may inform the source of your husband's death, and tell them it will be paid with the settlement of the estate. If the bill is in both names, or, of course, yours, pay it promptly. This may seem difficult in the midst of all you need to do, and the state of your emotions. However, it is a simple act that will aid you in the long run. Your credit score is affected by the timely payment of bills. On-time payments count for 35 percent of your credit score. Also, the less debt you owe on your cards, the better your score will be. If you must, at a later time, make a major purchase such as a car by borrowing funds, your interest rate will be affected by your credit score. If you have no credit history, securing one credit card, using it judiciously, and paying the entire balance before the deadline will start building your credit history.

Many widows are surprised to discover that they have little credit history. Bank accounts and credit cards may have been in their husband's name, and that worked fine while he was living. However, it may be difficult to open accounts or get a credit card in your name, given this circumstance. Having a credit history—a good one—is important in today's world. To check your credit score, go to www.experian.com, www.equifax.com, or www.transunion.com.

4. *Call Social Security to obtain survivor benefits.*

I found myself utilizing the Social Security Administration's

Web site. You may make an appointment and go to your local office, or in some cases accomplish what's necessary over the phone. If you and your husband were both collecting Social Security before, you will receive only the greater of the two benefits. If you are collecting retirement income from another government fund, you must choose one, as you cannot collect from both. In my case, I am not eligible for either my Social Security or my husband's because I am a retired public educator.

If you have children under eighteen years of age, you will receive assistance for them as well.

5. Find out how much you have in assets, and discover your liabilities as well.

Finding and organizing your financial documents can be simple, hard, surprising, and time consuming. Just remember, YES, YOU CAN!

One son, while helping his mother, e-mailed Widowconnection .com stating that it took one year for him to track down all his father's obscure investments after his death. Thank God for a persistent son!

Appendix F includes two forms to help you organize your finances and understand your financial situation more clearly. The List of Debts and the Financial Statement are also available for download at Widowconnection.com. There are a few sources that are helpful in the "finding" process: past tax returns, the benefits administrator at your husband's job, your husband's accountant or lawyer, and simply opening all the mail carefully. The benefits administrator should be able to explain the details of your husband's pension, 401(k), and life insurance plans.

It is not uncommon during this step to discover a new emotion creeping in alongside your grief, anxiety, and fear: anger. Oh, my dear sister, on this journey you may discover that your husband was overly optimistic, not practical, talked of a will but never made one, or any number of unpleasant to smelly surprises. You may be justifiably angry. You have reason to feel disillusioned. Your husband's choices may have hurt you. That is, however, the past. I have three suggestions:

◆ Go to his grave site or other meaningful location and talk it out—be real. Tell him what you know. Tell him how you wish things were. Scream, whisper, cry, or all three.

◆ Forgive. If you are a Christ-follower, remember that you have been forgiven much. His clay feet, clay wallet, and clay bank account are the results of his being human. It is unlikely that he created a mess for you on purpose.

◆ Roll up your sleeves, sharpen your pencil and your mind, and prayerfully move forward. Use that adrenaline to take step 6.

6. Organize all financial documents, getting your money house in order.

This can be fun. Your basic "organizational model" may be a box with inexpensive folders in your favorite color. Your method may be different than his, and your labels may be different. But it's your office now. What works for you? How can you put your hand quickly on your car insurance records? Are envelopes or accordion folders your way to save receipts? Create your financial records space. If you are doing this on your computer, paperless is good. Remember to save and back up files just in case.

7. Talk to other wise people about their choices, including appropriate VIPs on your board of directors, but make your own decisions.

We ask good cooks for their recipes; we ask financial advice from those who've done it right. Get information from lots of sources. Get references from friends and associates about good certified financial planners. I asked three different planners what they would do with a specific sum of money, given my needs and goals. The proposed plans I received were important information in making my choice. Before choosing a financial planner:

◆ Interview at least three.

◆ Check their reputation.

◆ Consider a fee-based CFP first (i.e., the advice they give is not based on their selling you a product).

◆ Be especially careful if considering a friend or relative.

How to interview a financial advisor:

The head of one international organization of financial advisors stated, "Nobody will watch out for your backside" and "Everyone wants to part you from your money." She has a "trust-no-one-until-they-earn-it" attitude.

Here are questions we need to ask:

◆ How, and how much are you paid? Are you paid a fee by me, or with a commission paid by a company for selling its product, or a combination thereof? If there is no fee and you are having trouble discovering how they benefit from your business, ask, "What transaction has to occur before you get paid?"

◆ Are you a fiduciary? Fiduciaries must put their clients' interests first, before their own. Brokers must select suitable investments for you. Certified planners are usually fiduciaries. Ask what their credentials are. Because someone has knowledge of personal finance does not mean they are ethical or have integrity. Belonging to a religious organization does not guarantee those qualities either. Get recommendations from many who are using an individual over a period of time before selecting one.

◆ Show me a plan of how you would invest $_____. Compare plans from at least three people.

◆ Then remember to:
    Check references.
    Be cautious in choosing a friend or relative.
    Never commit to someone who talks down to you.
    Require that they get previous approval from you.
    before moving money.
    Consider a fee-based CFP while getting started.
    Ask for names of clients with circumstances similar to yours that you may contact.

I found it helpful to read lots of financial papers and consumer magazines. Also talking with other widows about mistakes they've made, and hearing what they wish they had done differently, helps us sort our choices.

8. Reinvest your money.

If you are not ready to make long-term choices, park your money in a high-yielding CD until you are more comfortable making decisions. Often, life insurance companies will offer to put your money in an account and give you a checkbook to draw on that account. Your guaranteed interest rate will be low. I resisted the temptation of ease in order to opt for a higher return elsewhere. The lump disbursement box to check on life insurance policies is typically in small print in an obscure location. In my case, the salesman of the policy insisted that the check be mailed to him upon which he would bring it to me. (In other words, he wanted to sell me an annuity when he "delivered" my check.) I had to be quite forceful in order for the check to be mailed directly to me. This process added stress I certainly did not need at that time. Sadly, this person claimed to be a believer and is a "friend of a friend." He was not looking out for my needs, but was hoping to sell an expensive product to a widow, one I did not need. As I mentioned earlier, we as widows can discover we are very important to investment institutions and salespeople of their products.

Beware of new friends who are interested in your financial needs and future. Just because an individual worships where you do or is known by your friends does not make that person a sound or wise financial planner or investment advisor. Read, learn, and check the product and the person out. Though you might have missed earning some interest on your money by leaving it in a safe CD while you were educating yourself, remember that during that learning time you may have avoided putting money in an *unwise* place with high costs for moving it out to a place more appropriate for your needs.

9. Maintain your budget.

Congratulations! You've started. You can do this. You'll be amazed at the difference a few minutes a day will make in your financial life. Recording everything helps you stay focused. The end of the month becomes fun and satisfying, not a time to dread. Whatever you give up in temporary gratification is small as you sense your growing feeling of competence and security. You can put on that old sweater with a smile, knowing you are paying off a credit card or putting a little money in your IRA. You may make a fresh pot of coffee and take some in a travel mug for your road trip, whizzing by that expensive drive-through coffee shop you used to frequent. You smile as you visualize your balanced budget sheet!

I love learning new things to help me with my budget. Just this week I read something I had not heard before. I read that homeowners should spend 1–1.5 percent of the value of their home to maintain it each year. [6] In other words, if your home value is $200,000 you should expect to spend $2,000 to $3,000 on upkeep per year. Good to know. If you, like me, prefer knowledge to surprises, this bit of information helps us in creating and managing our budget.

Let's keep learning! Money miracles may not happen overnight. But you've started!

10. Reinvest as needed.

Just keep learning. Keep your eye on your money. No one else will examine your funds like you will. You will learn, grow more competent, and thrive with your new wisdom. Here are a few more interesting facts:

Since our average age is a little over fifty-five,[7] we have approximately thirty years to perfect our skills!

There are twelve million widows in the United States today, and there are three million widowers.

52 percent of workers 55 and over have less than $50,000 in savings[8]

Estimated assets held by Americans 65 and older come to $15 trillion, the most in history for that age group. These assets are held by a small percent of that age group.

You may be in neither category. But you can be a member of the successful YES, YOU CAN widows group. The buck that stops with you will be well managed.

A BIBLICAL PERSPECTIVE ON FINANCES

Money is referenced many times in Scripture: 114 times in the New International Version, 125 times in the King James Version, and 134 times in the New American Standard Bible. If you expand the word *money* to include all we own, there are several thousand references to "stuff," what is truly ours, and what's His. Widows are referenced 103 times in Scripture. Both are important to God. Therefore, it's important for us as widows to learn God's heart on our finances.

Since there are many good general books on biblical stewardship and finances, I'll focus here on Scripture particularly meaningful to us.

You may have a favorite widow story in Scripture. My top two are the ones of the widow's mite, and of the widow and her pot of oil. Excuse me if I sound like I'm preaching a sermon, but I so love these two women and am looking forward to "setting a spell" with them in heaven and learning their whole life stories.

The custom of giving in the New Testament was a public one. People walked up to a container, depositing their gift in a way that all could see who gave and how much. In this incident Jesus had just warned in His teachings to "Watch out for the teachers of the law. They like to walk around in flowing robes and be greeted in the marketplaces, and have the most important seats in the synagogues and the places of honor at banquets. They devour widows' houses and for a show make lengthy prayers. Such men will be punished most severely" (Mark 12:38–40).

A present-day example might be one who forecloses on a widow's home, or counsels her to make an investment for his profit, not hers. And then, having lined his pockets with her money, made a noisy, large gift to the church, and prayed loudly thanking God for his prosperity.

Following that teaching, Jesus sat down opposite the treasury for a visual of His teaching.

> Jesus sat down opposite the place where the offerings were put and watched the crowd putting their money into the temple treasury. Many rich people threw in large amounts. But a poor widow came and put in two very small copper coins, worth only a fraction of a penny. Calling his disciples to him, Jesus said, "I tell you the truth, this poor widow has put more into the treasury than all the others. They all gave out of their wealth; but she, out of her poverty, put in everything—all she had to live on." (Mark 12:41–44)

She made music to the heart of God.

She was generous beyond expectation, authentic by investing in what she treasured, and did not care that her two mites made little noise rolling down that treasury receptacle. But she made music to the heart of God. This woman's actions—though she herself was invisible in the places of power in the synagogue—has been told of around the world through every decade, every century, because of her generosity. To say more is unnecessary. I love to learn of someone who raises the bar for all of us.

This second story is special because we see God providing for a widow using a method that involved community and faith.

> The wife of a man from the company of the prophets cried out to Elisha, "Your servant my husband is dead, and you know that he revered the Lord. But now his creditor is coming to take my two boys as his slaves." Elisha replied to her, "How can I help you? Tell me, what do you have in your house?" "Your servant has nothing there at all," she said, "except a little oil." Elisha said, "Go around and ask all your neighbors for empty jars. Don't ask for just a few. Then go inside and shut the door behind you and your sons. Pour oil into all the jars, and as each

is filled, put it to one side." She left him and afterward shut the door behind her and her sons. They brought the jars to her and she kept pouring. When all the jars were full, she said to her son, "Bring me another one." But he replied, "There is not a jar left." Then the oil stopped flowing. She went and told the man of God, and he said, "Go, sell the oil and pay your debts. You and your sons can live on what is left." (2 Kings 4:1–7)

Imagine the scene as the widow's sons hurry around the neighborhood borrowing jars. Do the neighbors know the miracle coming? Not yet, but they will. Imagine the impact on these young men, knowing slavery would have been their next stage in life. Imagine the three of them behind that closed door watching the oil roll. The whole scene is beyond my comprehension in our culture of such wealth. When I shared this Scripture with an assembly of over two hundred widows in Ouagadougou, Burkina Faso, they understood. Imagine the witness that raced through the neighborhood streets when the sons returned the neighbors' pots after selling the oil on the market! Imagine the mark on these boys' lives, seeing the miracle that literally purchased their freedom. I read this story and am in awe, once again, at how God loves us and provides for us in surprising ways. I can add nothing. Others can watch Him in action as He protects us and keeps His promises. The question for us is, "How can we respond?" Only one answer is appropriate: Be generous and be faith-filled.

Charity begins not because we have deep pockets, but because of our love of giving. To whom should you give? That is between you and your Creator. Needs you notice all around you may be opportunities for you to be generous: to invest time in tutoring students in need, to give to your place of worship, to help any organization that promotes faith or well-being in your community, to be a driver for the disabled. Opportunities are endless.

The moment your heart is open to giving, an opportunity will appear.

Section Two

A Widow's Strengths

Chapter Four

Our OPPORTUNITY
TO CHANGE:
Free Time and Flexibility

———∞∞∞———

"A ship is safe in harbor, but that's not what ships are for."
—WILLIAM SHEDD

THE SWEET, GENTLE
CURRENT OF FREEDOM RISING

*I*n chapter 1, we explained our solitary, terrible, unpredictable, indefinable journey through waves of grief. Just as we might think we gained our sea legs to upright ourselves, an undertow would suck us under. What prompted that rogue wave? The scent of his aftershave? But we're in a store, and he is not here. Where did the undertow come from? We open an unexpected bill, and we were wondering before the bill if our finances were okay. The current of grief seemed to rule our emotions, our calendar, our total existence as days stretched into weeks and then into months after our loss. The current of grief took us at will on its secret timetable against our wishes. And the current of grief took us where we did not want to go. Financial uncertainties and fear made us vulnerable.

I describe those months of my life as blank. Some widows define them by a color, usually grey, sometimes black. Tomorrow was an unknown. The only sure thing was that there would be surprises, most of them unwelcome. While the powerful currents that make us vulnerable seem to be the only force in our lives, in reality, something else is happening. It begins in those early solitary months almost imperceptibly. It is the sweet, gentle current of freedom.

Did we want this freedom? No. Would we gladly give it up to have our husband back? Yes. But we did not get to choose. This freedom is now ours whether we want it or not. I was taken quite by surprise at this presence of freedom in my new life. At first I was angry to have it. I did not want all the choices—from the mundane ones in the grocery store, to the setting of the bedside alarm, to choosing a new vehicle. Who cares? I cry. I want the stability, the sameness, the comfort of my past life—not to mention wanting my husband back.

But that life is no longer an option. And I feel this new current again. It is slow and gentle, and its direction is determined by the choices I make. Of necessity I begin to choose my schedule for the day. I begin to choose what I will do about my health. I begin to choose what I will do with my spare time. There is a trickle of pleasure at being able to control something of my life again. The sense of *having* to choose (ugh) is changing to *getting* to choose (smile). Finally a positive surprise I can welcome!

TRANSITIONS: READY OR NOT

"Don't make any big decisions for at least two years." Caring friends repeat the advice they've heard and they are right. Whatever the cause of huge change in one's life, it is not a good time to make consequential decisions. However, life is never static. One can't push a pause button on life and have it stand still until your wounds are at least scarred over enough so you can think straight. Some decisions must be made, and even though small, those decisions do start us on a direction in our new life. They matter. So how do we navigate through this transition?

I compare this transition part of the journey to a hike in the mountains. We embark on our hike looking around us to assess what's ahead. We see range layered upon range. Sometimes the finish point is hidden from view. My transition time had an ironic aspect to it as well. Let me explain.

I decided to study Scripture about transitions.

In the spring of 2003, I knew I would be retiring from my career in high school counseling in June of 2006. During that season, I decided to study Scripture about transitions. My intent was to navigate the change with comfort, wisdom, and some degree of purpose. I had started teaching a university class in the evening to explore if that might be my next career. Never one to be without a plan for my life, I thought all could be organized if you open the Word and apply your mind to the situation. I studied great people in the Bible to examine what they did, and how they behaved in times of significant change.

That summer, in the process of my study, I was asked to share a devotional with the spouses of the managers of the Moody Broadcasting Network's owned and operated stations. We were meeting in the Gatlinburg area of Tennessee. I asked if I could do the devotional somewhere along the path of a hike we had decided to take. Perfect, I thought; my topic on transitions would be shared in the mountains.

Our group chattered and laughed, climbed and paused, chattered more, climbed higher, and eventually decided it was break time. We settled on rocks around a gentle waterfall. With Tennessee summertime wetting our foreheads, we cooled our feet in the deep puddles and drained our water bottles. In this setting I shared what I was learning about transitions. And of course, I told them why I was studying the topic—my upcoming retirement from public education. Not many miles away, my healthy husband was playing a round of golf with his friends.

My Bible practically fell open to the dog-eared pages describing the lives of the people I was examining. The passages seemed relevant to seemingly everyone in our hiking group, people who were facing job changes, geographical moves, empty nests; including the one other soon-to-be-retired public educator.

Abraham moved forward into the unknown. And he did not know what the next move would be. But God did make it clear to him he was to move (Genesis 12). Consider Moses. Even though he was 120 years old, his eyesight was not dimmed and he was still vigorous; he was physically capable of leading the children of Israel into the Promised Land. So Moses could do the job. But obviously, God had a different plan. Yes, Moses had given up the privilege of finishing the job by his missteps and sin earlier. But there is still more to the picture here. Don't you sense that God in His overarching plan was looking at Joshua? This young man was to be the next leader of the children of Israel. Did God not see the stature of the person Joshua needed to become for his tasks ahead? Did God not know the timetable of when the leadership baton needed to be passed on to the next person? (See Deuteronomy 34.)

It wasn't all about Moses. God has a bigger picture and a grander plan than we can calculate. Transition is not all about us. It's not all about me. We surely think so and in our myopia wish so. But it is *not all about me*. As our group studied this together, the incredible view drew us into the distance. Though we could see the next mountain, the valley between us and the next ridge was too low for the eye to follow the path and discern whether it was smooth, overgrown, crisscrossed with streams, or dry.

And then there was Elijah. You just have to love Elijah. A guy who dresses weird, has an unrewarding job of telling people what they don't want to hear, and becomes the enemy of a powerful, violent woman. Who would want this job? He is the attention-getting, miracle-performing prophet who can bring down fire on a soaked altar. When his star power peaks and he is the national buzz, he's running away to hide from the queen, who's bent on revenge! Talk about transitions. Then following his flamboyant season he becomes the quiet teacher of a school of prophets. Transitions again—big-time. (Read the story in 1 Kings 18–19.)

This story confirms again the lesson of Moses. It's not about what I *can* do. Moses could still lead. Elijah could still do astounding miracles and prophesy. But God was choosing to change his job description. And Elisha, who would be Elijah's replacement, was in the learning trenches. Once again we get a sense that God is thinking about Elisha and the skills and experience he would need for the next season.

God decides to replace Elijah as well. To read 2 Kings 2 is to read a most tender tale of the young Elisha yearning to follow in the footsteps of his mentor. He keeps stride with his teacher/friend, not wishing to miss receiving his mantle of blessing. Did Elijah get it right? With the incredible changes in what God asked him to do, did Elijah miss the mark? God answers these questions by sending "a chariot of fire and horses of fire" to lift Elijah from this earth and escort him to a place more beautiful, joy filled, and peace filled than we can imagine. No hunger, fatigue, Jezebels, whiners, pretenders— and a chariot sent by God to take him there. I'd say Elijah got it right.

Everything changes. It's not about us, it's not about what we can do, it's not about what we have done. It's all about God.

Our times are in His hands.

Our job description is in His hands.

It's all about Him.

> *He tells us in Scripture*
> *that widows have a*
> *special place in His heart.*

Our group shares with one another the transitions we know we are facing in our lives. We pray. The pleasant murmur of the water from the falls over the rocks around us whispers God's *Amen* to our petitions and our thanksgiving. We collect the trappings of our hike and start the descent. My friend and soon-to-be-retired educator Jan, unbeknownst to me, picks up a rock from the waterfall as a memoir of the moment and the lesson. And here I am today, in the fifth spring after I embarked on the study of transitions in the Bible. I pick up that rock and run my fingers over the etched reminder from my friend Jan: "The Smokies, 2003." God knew I needed to be digging. He knew I needed to be learning. He knew that my retirement would be the smallest transition of the many of these past five years.

I tell you this story not just for the lessons Scripture teaches us about transitions, but to show you that God does have His hand on you as a treasured person. He tells us in Scripture that widows have a special place in His heart. His gentle guidance of me in this study before I became a widow reminded me that He knew ahead of time the journey I would be on. He knows the mountains and valleys we each must walk. He was gently assuring me that He would make sure I made it through.

Now that I'm armed with the knowledge that my successful transition is not dependent on what I have done in the past, or what I can do in the present, what can I lean on to help me through? While we know that God can do anything with our future regardless of our past, He usually builds on some of our previous strengths.

What were your strengths and skills before you became a widow? What were some of your positive personal habits before you became a widow? Were you orderly, good at gathering information, inclined to go to the Bible for help? Were you good at managing money? Writing down these personal strengths can be helpful.

> My past positive personal habits including living and health matters
> My past positive personal habits related to money
> My past positive personal habits related to communicating with others

Some of our strengths and skills were either used in jobs we've had or developed through our work and career experience. Let's examine them.

> What jobs have you had in the past?
> What were the skills you used on each job?

Job # 1 _____

Skills used in Job # 1 _____

_____

_____

_____

Job # 2 _____

Skills used in Job # 2 _____

_____

_____

_____

What restricted you in previous jobs? Often, marital constraints of your husband's schedule, geographical necessity of his job, family, or other aspects are no longer factors in your new life today. This can be a positive new freedom.

Restrictions in previous jobs _____

_____

Many women have developed skills through volunteer work. In marriage, volunteerism might have been done together as a couple or individually. Regardless of whether you volunteered as a couple or alone, you brought something to the project and probably grew because of the opportunity. List some of the volunteer work you have done and the skills you used in them.

Volunteer task # 1 _____

Skills used in volunteer task # 1 _____

_____

_____

_____

Volunteer task # 2 _____

Skills used in volunteer task # 2 _____
_____
_____
_____

What restricted you in previous volunteer efforts? Again, sometimes time constraints or geographical constraints dictated your efforts.

Restrictions in previous volunteer projects _____
_____
_____
_____

It is not unusual for widows to discover that opportunities, such as a short-term international missions trip, for example, that were out of the question during their married life are now a possibility. Juggling work and vacation schedules, as well as passions for different projects, may have ruled out opportunities in the past that you now find appealing. Is the sweet, gentle current of freedom beginning to lift the edges of your soul? Let's continue. You have likely had more than two jobs and volunteered on more than two projects. Continue the lists in a notebook until you feel you have a comprehensive list of the skills you have used.

The next step is a bit more visionary and can be more fun.

Now, what would you *like* to do? Okay, dream. Just write it down.

Start your own business.

Tutor elementary students at risk.

Learn to develop a Web page.

Tutor adults so they can pass the Graduate Equivalency Degree exam.

Become computer literate (be able to send and receive e-mail, research products on the Internet, and more).

Sell or buy real estate (you may have to pay to play, but you don't have to pay to learn; check around for classes).

Create stained glass artwork.

Learn about investments, stock markets, and mutual funds.

Go to law school.

Learn to appeal your property taxes.

Become certified at scuba diving.

Run for an office in your town (school board, trustee, etc.).

Work in a coffee shop.

Sell your junk on eBay.

Work in a bookstore or library.

Learn to play one video game with your grandchildren.

Travel.

Encourage other widows you know.

Take a course at your local college or junior college.

Take a class at your church.

Learn to polka.

You'll think of endless opportunities that interest you.

You'll think of endless opportunities that interest you. Don't rule out anything at this time. Begin to explore the dreams that spark your interest. As a new widow you may need a nudge of some sort to get you started. I did. I'll tell you what motivated me to get started looking forward.

I decided to follow in my husband's footsteps on a few projects he had pursued. While we had traveled over the United States and to over forty other countries as his broadcast vision and professional opportunities grew, there were a few places I had missed.

These were projects I had not been able to share with him due to my full-time job and other responsibilities.

Bob had been instrumental in starting a radio station in the Angola prison in Louisiana. I recalled him returning from his first visit to the prison visibly changed in his perception of incarceration and his compassion for inmates and their families. I knew something was going to happen. (There were several such experiences in our forty-one years of marriage where I observed Bob not only become aware of a need, but at some visceral level put his hand to the plow. Something would happen, or he would die trying.) Radio station KLSP was birthed, the first "incarceration station" to my knowledge. I wanted to follow in Bob's footsteps to Angola and see his work.

While KLSP is a miracle worth writing about, and I was changed as was Bob by visiting Angola, the purpose of my writing here is not about this meaningful project. Rather than describing the trip and the relevance of this project, I'd like to share the trip's impact on me as a new widow. What was right about the trip was that I actively took the first step to do something I had never done before. If you happen to be reading this and you are *not* a widow, this may seem so simple and inconsequential that it comes across as a silly statement. If you are a widow, you understand. In our state of seeing the world as grey or blank, in our state of numbness, in our "nothing matters" life, it is easier to do nothing. Sometimes picking up the phone is like trying to bench-press a hundred pounds. I'd encourage you to just do it. You never just step through an open door—you must first reach for the knob, turn it, and see if the door will open for you.

Your hand, your tired hand, your numb hand, your hand that is wishing for the touch of your gentleman to open the door for you, is now the only hand you have. Remember, I've been there; I understand; and your hand is stronger than you think.

In talking to other widows, I have discovered that I am not alone in wanting to follow in my husband's footsteps or perhaps retrace steps we took together. From my experience, as well as listening to others, here are some of the joys you'll experience, as well as some of the feelings that might catch you off guard.

There is a joy in connecting with your husband's presence in a different place. It is common for us as widows to wish somehow to sense the reality of our husband. We miss him so much. The void he has left is so huge, so vacant, so unfillable. It's normal to wish somehow to discover something of him somewhere to put a little something in that void. You'll wonder, will I talk to someone who remembers him? Will they tell me some bit of a story I had not heard before? Will my eyes rest on something he saw? Will I sense his perception of what I'm seeing? After all, they say married people begin to look alike over time. I think we also see alike, meaning that we observe and perceive things in a similar way over time.

All of these things happened at the Angola prison, and I was comforted. I shared Bob's joy at the good things that were happening there. I talked to inmates who had talked to Bob. Yes, the joy is sweet, but it is accompanied by other emotions.

Be prepared for pangs of sadness to unexpectedly invade your space. The finality of my loss moved in on my feelings in Angola. I was seeing a dream he started but could no longer experience. I was seeing new inmates who would never know Bob. Could he have continued to put his powerful hand to the plow in forward motion and start stations in other prisons? I will never know. I do know that the trip initiated another adventure for me. I traveled to San Quentin, California, and met spiritual brothers there who are incarcerated. This has been a blessing I would never have anticipated upon entering this transition time.

Following our husband's footsteps, we also see that life moves on. A part of us resists that strenuously. We want his friends to still vividly remember him and speak of him. We want the presence of his smile to be real around every corner. Retracing his steps, the reality of the world moving on is in our face. Still, the joy outweighed the pain. I scheduled one more trip.

My husband had traveled to Burkina Faso and Côte d'Ivoire (formerly Ivory Coast), Africa, to partner with broadcasters there. My son Rob traveled with him, as did friends from HCJB, an international broadcasting group. He began a partnership with Lee and Michele Sonius, missionaries in Africa and with broadcaster Joanna Ilboudo. This was one trip I was fortunate to have missed. Their plane to depart Ouagadougou, Burkina Faso, was cancelled, making necessary a twenty-six-hour bus ride accompanied by goats and chickens. Soldiers frequently stopped their bus for "checks," and a nasty midnight tire explosion further slowed progress, testing the patience and humor of the group. Within two weeks after they arrived home, war broke out between the two countries. This explained the frequent boardings by the soldiers and heightened my gratitude that they were home safe.

Ouagadougou seemed like a place I should visit. I e-mailed the Soniuses, whom I had never met, and asked if I could visit them. I don't think missionaries ever say no. My friend Pat Jacquin at HCJB wanted to go as well and was willing to make the arrangements. Such a deal! Sonius not only would house us in Ghana, but Michele would join us for the trip to Ouagadougou, and Joanna was willing to take us around Burkina Faso. Six months after Bob left for heaven, I was on my way to Africa to retrace his footsteps.

One other change had happened in the meantime. Joanna had resigned as a radio station manager and started a ministry to widows and orphans. This change resulted in a total transformation of the lessons I would learn on this trip. When Joanna e-mailed me telling me of her new position, she asked if I would teach from the Bible to widows groups she would assemble. Do people who love to share from the Bible ever say no? Not me! While I would have been shocked to be asked to stand in front of a group here in the United States such a short time after Bob's home-going, somehow doing this a continent away made it feel doable.

I began my preparation at the computer by asking for a printout of every verse in the Bible that included the word *widow*. I found 113 references. I wanted to share with the widows in Africa what God's heart was for them. I was rewarded by the rich experience of exploring an aspect of God I never knew. Wanting to be prepared for whatever Joanna asked of me, I prepared several messages. A new sense in my soul caught me off guard, pleasantly this time. It was a sense of eagerness.

If you are a new widow reading this, you may not have noticed that your sense of positive expectation for the next day has disappeared. What this felt like to me was, "Why a new day?" "Why a tomorrow?" This is the "blank," the "grey" of our emotions. We lose the eager anticipation of a new tomorrow. I understand. If you, like me, experienced an extended time with your husband's terminal illness, it seems that the dread of tomorrow goes on forever even before you become a widow. This is normal. We have not lost our minds. We have not lost our faith. We are simply getting through each day as well as we can.

You can imagine what a sweet surprise it was for me to sense eagerness in my being! I had never before thought of positive anticipation as such a blessing. It was an expected, taken for granted part of life. No more. Eagerness is a gift. How can I describe my trip to Africa? While I had been to Egypt and Morocco, Ghana and Burkina Faso were quite different. I gained a different perspective on the economic aspects of those countries. I gained a different understanding of the AIDS epidemic. In some ways, my worldview changed. But those issues are beyond the purposes of this book. What was of value as a widow that I can share with you? There were at least three precious truths that going to Africa taught me: We are more resilient than we think; new friends will be discovered in new ways and in new places; and God is creative in His plan for us.

1. WE ARE MORE RESILIENT THAN WE THINK.

Do you already have a concept of your capabilities? Scratch it. Do you already have a concept of your ability to stretch and adapt to new situations? Pitch it. You have changed, whether you know it or not. I could share example after example just from this one trip. Selectively here are a few.

GOD'S DAY, HIS CALENDAR
This is the day the Lord has made; let us rejoice and be glad in it.
(Psalm 118:24)

My first speaking engagement went as planned. I was to speak to a group of widows at a church. Joanna and I stood at our microphones, and she translated as I began to teach about the widow and her pot of oil (2 Kings 4). These widows understood poverty, not having enough. They understood their children being at risk with no father. The sea of faces, the brightly colored dresses, and the intensity in their eyes communicated to me that God's lesson was relevant for widows everywhere. I was in awe and humbled beyond words to see God at work on this sweltering afternoon.

After the lesson, prayer, and singing, we prepared to leave. Joanna spoke to the women in leadership from the church, who said that they would be back the next day. The next afternoon, the crowd was larger, possibly three hundred people. I was able to look carefully at the women. Many looked so young. Some leaned forward as they listened. These were hungry, intentional learners. I wish I could say I was so Spirit-filled that I had no awareness of the mundane of the moment. However, I will admit that as I felt sweat literally run down the calves of my legs into my sandals, I knew that hundreds of people under a metal roof under the African sun is one warm meeting.

At the conclusion of the afternoon, these African women did something that we often do here at the conclusion of women's retreats. They took turns standing and sharing what the sessions had meant to them. Joanna translated for me. I was not surprised to find that they found great courage from the truths of Scripture about widows. We are assured that when we share Scripture, the Word works. (His Word will not return void.) There was, however, something surprising to me that several of them shared. They gained strength from the timing of my visit. Many stated that they were surprised that so soon after losing my husband, I could travel to them to teach. Their response to this was that if I could do that, they could be strong too. The timing of the trip had been a surprise and a puzzle to me, but planned and timed by God for His purposes.

GOD'S GROUP: JUST SHOW UP

One of our outings took us on an eighty-kilometer trip outside the city of Ouagadougou to a remote village. I call it remote not because of the great distance, but because of the driving conditions.

Perhaps one-third of the distance was on a paved highway. Then Joanna took a turn onto what I would consider an off-roading adventure . . . except that we were not in a Hummer. We were in an aging station wagon that had several issues, one of which was a nonfunctioning air-conditioning system. This was of negligible importance, though, as the most important thing now was functioning tires and visibility. Usually I could determine where the road was; in fact, sometimes it was a quite narrow path through grasses taller than the car. As there were multiple sharp turns, I imagined another vehicle careering around a bend directly into us. This was quite a far-fetched fear. We never saw another vehicle from the time we left the highway. The only other means of travel were the occasional donkeys we saw tied to a tree or shrub.

We drove through the countryside with Joanna leaning forward to see around the twists and turns. I leaned forward too, as if that would help. Eventually we emerged from the grasses upon a large group of brightly clad men, women, and children singing and clapping. They were out in force to greet us. We joined them and walked on up the road to their village. We received a tour that included the grinding stone in the middle of the huts, large water containers that they filled by walking to a distant well, and the pastor's porch—a patch of earth covered with thatch to protect us from the sun.

After the appropriate pleasantries, the pastor led us into their church where the meeting would take place. As everyone began to file in, we became aware this was not a widows-only meeting. Teens arrived and seated themselves in one area. The women filed in on one side, the men on another, and all the children in the front. There were many more women than men due to the AIDS epidemic. The church was packed. As Pat, my friend from HCJB, and Michele prayed, I shuffled notes and changed my illustrations from Scripture to include Benaiah and Elijah, as well as the widow and her jug of oil.

As I rose to speak, I had to intentionally put aside a distracting thought. Before we entered, the pastor had pointed out a man tied to a tree outside the village because he was demon-possessed. While I had many theological questions about this practice, now was not the time to mull them over. I prayed for clarity and shared from the Word.

Afterward we went back to the pastor's porch. Their leaders prayed for us and told each of us what their visions were for our individual futures. The pastor pronounced his blessing on what I shared. "It is good," was his declaration. Then they proceeded to give us gifts of dried okra, spices, and a live goat. Our attempts to explain that we could not accept the goat would not be heard. Upon our exit, the goat was bound and placed in the back of the station wagon, bleating loudly in protest. Off we went on our journey back to the highway. Occasionally the goat would stop bleating. We would chatter, forgetting he was there. Then something would prompt him to bawl again, causing us to jump in our seats.

The gifts we gave
were minuscule compared
to what we received.

At the end of the day, we decided to "regift" the goat to another village. We were humbled at the generosity of a village that looked and lived much like the villages I saw pictured in the *National Geographic* when I was a child. Fifty years had not brought prosperity to this harsh land. But harsh living had not shrunk the giving spirit of a village who just appreciated people showing up. The gifts we gave were minuscule compared to what we received. I was learning that we are more resilient than we think. It's a pleasant discovery.

Another lesson from Africa was a quite pleasant one about friendships:

2. NEW FRIENDS WILL BE DISCOVERED
IN NEW WAYS AND IN NEW PLACES.

When Bob and I traveled through Eastern Europe, Spain, and Morocco with Dick and Pat Jacquin, I enjoyed their easy friendship enormously. Bob had traveled with Dick before and they enjoyed a mutual professional respect, friendship, and, I might add, bizarre humor. I was delighted to get to know Pat, and I expected we would enjoy many more trips as couples.

This was not to be, due to Bob's illness. I never imagined that Pat would become my travel buddy. When she was not only up for the trip to Africa, but willing to manage all the details, I was thrilled. But in our travels I discovered a larger treasure in our woman-to-woman friendship. In our foursome, I had not discovered the extent of her spiritual discernment, and her communication skill and calm in front of large, ever-changing groups. I discovered her competence under pressure, her ability to never let surprises distract her from accomplishing the task at hand. In short, I discovered another woman of depth whom I might never have known in our couple friendship. We intend to take more trips and might find more avenues for our friendship.

Michele's friendship was another surprise. Traveling without her husband with two other women was a first for her. It was her first trip to Burkina Faso as well. Born to missionaries in Africa and committed to serving there as well, her thirst to learn was refreshing. I was enriched by her perspectives as we adventured our way through visits to villages, tours of medical clinics, church ser-vices and widows meetings. By the end of our trip I knew we could travel and serve together. While I do not know if God has that in our future, I would welcome it.

Why do I tell you these new friend stories? To encourage you that unexpected, new relationships will be happening in your life. Mine were from unexpected connections that never would have happened in my life as a married person. Yours probably will be as well. When you are open to new adventures, new friendships are likely to happen in the process. Part of that gentle current of freedom you feel is the ability to discover new blessings in some relationships from the past. Your new singleness will also bring other people into your life.

3. GOD IS CREATIVE IN HIS PLAN FOR US.

The return flight over the Atlantic was not one of those "just sleep through it" flights. My mind tried to wrap itself around the experiences of the past days. Following in Bob's footsteps turned out to be as much about discovering a new Miriam as it was retracing his steps. Recording a radio program with Joanna in the RED FM 93.4 studio where he had recorded, seeing a bus like the one of his long twenty-six-hour ride from Burkina Faso to Ivory Coast, meeting the radio people he had met, were bittersweet moments.

The moments of sweet without the bitter were stepping up to a microphone again with eager anticipation. In one instance it was a crowd of five churches holding a joint meeting. I had never spoken with five pastors sitting behind me in those imposing huge chairs. But I was eager and not afraid. Pondering my role in helping widows in the future and remembering the mental images of the widows making soap at all the widow villages prompted another new emotion—anticipation of a purposeful life in the future. How could one sleep with possibilities churning through one's brain?

Let me encourage you to take some real steps of action trying out the unknown.

I had set off on the trip with one goal. More than mission accomplished, I saw afresh that our creative God has a plan for our new life. He may unfold it bit by bit, or in large surprising chunks. Whatever His method, His plan is good. Walk into it.

I WILL, I AM, I CAN

Have you ever listened with weariness to someone proclaiming that you can do anything you want to do? You can be anything you wish to be. And as they speak louder and the crowd responds more, they shout, "You can, You can, You can!"

And then the meeting is over, everyone leaves, you go back

home, and everyone and everything remains the same. I would be doing you a disservice, dear widow, if I summarized this chapter with just talk. Let me encourage you instead to take some real steps of action trying out the unknown. No, you needn't sail a catamaran, visit a prison, or travel to Africa, though I highly recommend them all. I can't tell you what that new thing in your life is. But it is probably whispering in your ear right now. Maybe it's learning to drive when you're sixty-five. Maybe it's sitting for a new certification. Let your mind roam. You'll only discover you can when you are in motion. So take that first step.

Chapter Five

We COMFORT OTHERS, and Comfort Comes Back

⸺⁂⸺

"How wonderful it is that nobody need wait a
single moment before starting to improve the world."
—ANNE FRANK

The farmhouse of my childhood had an attic that could
have been the stage set for the spookiest of dramas. When
you opened the hallway door on the main floor, you came
upon narrow stairs with a sharp turn that led to "the
attic." I know of no reason why the large room at the top
was unfinished. A dormer window had gaps to the outside
around the sills. Winter's wind blew in snow. Ice would
eventually build up, closing the gap when a big freeze followed melting snow or cold rain. Next to the window was
the strange shape of a closet-to-be. A heavy piece of plastic draped across the intended door. A howling wind outside set that plastic to moving and rattling. Ice etched
lines on the window like grasping long fingernails of a
frozen outside being that wanted in.

Doors on opposite sides of this room opened into cozy,
small misshapen rooms, rooms dictated and defined by
rooflines that, again, followed no reason. These were our
bedrooms. My older two sisters occupied one. It seemed

miles away as we were separated by "the attic."

A cold winter's night would find me bounding up the stairs in my long flannel nightgown and bare feet. The cold floor increased my speed as did the wailing sighs of the wind in the dormer and the cold blue ice framing the window. If little girls could fly, I did in those moments to the door to my room. Quick open, quick close—it was a bit warmer in here—and then dive! into my featherbed. If one could land on a cloud, it would feel like this. Softly I sank into the gentlest of spaces, feeling my comforter wrap around and conform to my shape. My feet were soon toasty and the cold of the attic banished to another universe. This was comfort.

I look back on the season of my husband's illness as life in the attic. Only another widow knows the icy fingers that grip one's soul, whether death comes quickly or approaches one month at a time. Has it taken a year? For Bob it was three years. It was attic time for my soul.

IN THE ATTIC

The reality for all of us is this: After our loss we want comfort. We crave the peace it brings. We hunger for comfort to fill the voids in our world and in us. Lasting comfort eludes us as long as we stay in the attic. After our husband leaves this earth, we must decide how long we will stay in that room. Will this be our permanent residence? If we stay, the essence of the woman God created can never emerge. The value of that woman can never be fully invested into others in her new life as a widow. She will seek comfort in selfish ways, if not destructive. I understand the temptation. In my attic, I thought, "Who cares? Why bother with the effort to exit? I'll just settle in; my attic is forever."

No doubt, in the first months, we feel it will be forever. We don't have the strength to exit, to even turn one door handle. We see no options. But choices are there. Eventually we see them. No one can take us from the attic. We must leave on our own steam to a new room—no, a new world—of our choosing.

How does this happen? How can we make this happen? Here were the voices I heard during my days in the attic.

"You need to take care of yourself." This was a truth I often heard as I cared for Bob during his battle with ALS. It was a truth I could not act on for the most part. There just weren't enough hours in the day. After he left, I did not know where to begin, or how. Again, it was truth, but it was months before I began to know what I needed to do for myself in my search for comfort. One widow in my ALS support group voiced a part of what I was feeling.

"I'm in the grocery store. I don't know what to buy. I don't even know what food I like. For years, I shopped for us and for him. What do I like? I don't know." Another expressed that she could not go back to the restaurants she frequented with her husband. One sold their vacation home and did not even return for the closing.

The comfort I craved was simply knowing I would be okay.

Most of us must find new activities, new places, new missions, ministries, and hobbies, to name a few of the important sources of comfort in our new life. We are all so different. What do we expect will bring comfort? Financial security? Good health? Connection to at least a few good friends and family? We see widows who have all that and are still not at peace, not experiencing what we're looking for. During my search, since I am a believer, one verse would regularly invade my mind: "Praise be to the God and Father of our Lord Jesus Christ, the Father of compassion and the God of all comfort, who comforts us in all our troubles, so that we can comfort those in any trouble with the comfort we ourselves have received from God" (2 Corinthians 1:3–4).

It seemed to me at that time that comfort would come from two sources:

- ◆ Those things I did for myself
- ◆ Something God would give me as a gift that was somehow

connected and possibly dependent on my passing it forward, regifting it to some other person in need

Frankly, I did not care much for either of those answers. I wanted some person with skin on, in my world, to bring comfort to me, to make it happen. That was not to be.

I knew from somewhere inside me that the comfort I craved was simply knowing I would be okay. I knew that if I had that soul satisfaction, I could sink into that featherbed of comfort and be at peace. So how do we find that comfort that moves us out of the attic? What I share about finding comfort is not only from my own journey, but what many have shared with me. Many women (and men) have shared their stories, and I pass on what they have discovered as well. Having now left the attic (okay, so I occasionally enter for a look back in time to the importance of that room in my life), I have concluded that our comfort depends on three things. A foundation and two vital pillars: taking care of ourselves and reaching out to others. Let's look at these three.

Our Foundation

Our foundation is a simple belief that God is, that He knew about the attic, that He was there with us in the attic, and that it is His loving intent that we not stay there. Our simple belief is that He is Good. I have, in fact, taken to saying, He is Grand (a statement that two years ago, during my husband's very difficult illness, I would have never even imagined I could dream of saying). This simple belief opens His hand to give us comfort that is not explainable in human terms. It is not measurable by psychological instruments, and it is not dependent on our circumstances. Our belief in Him unleashes His power to comfort us beyond description or measure.

The pillar of taking care of ourselves

Let's look at how can we take care of ourselves. What dangers might we encounter in our self-care that might keep us in the attic? The essential self-care aspects are our health, creation of a good

rhythm in our new life, and behavior that matches our spiritual principles. I'm still working on losing the extra twenty-five pounds I
found while consuming comfort foods during Bob's illness. Caregivers' bodies are typically overtaxed, and some muscles strained.
My swimming regimen has helped me recover. I have braces on my
teeth, an exercise schedule; and I actively prioritize walks, down-
times, and getaways to restore my body after three years of caregiv-
ing, and five of grieving. Rather than it being selfish, this is surviving.

God only gives us one body. We can replace some parts, but
not all. We cannot treat these bodies like used cars to be abandoned
or scrapped when wrecked, and expect God to give us a replacement. The temple of the Holy Spirit deserves better.

But a word of caution here. If comfort means consuming a
quart of Moose Tracks ice cream, then it's self-destructive. If comfort means a shopping spree on a maxed-out credit card—or any
useless purchases, for that matter—that behavior is self-destructive.
I have found that the activity that comforts my soul is not the fre-
netic busyness to drown my grief and sorrow, but a satisfying stroll
seeing God's creation today. Grief and sadness accompany me, but
feeling the spring breeze promising a new season ahead puts a
bounce in my step and clears my head.

Another word of caution is important here. Do not expect another *person* to be your source of comfort. While this important
topic might belong in a To Date or Not To Date section, I include
it here because I see widows and some widowers, in their vulnerability, hurting themselves by expecting someone else to bring them
comfort. One relatively young widow recognized that her finances
weren't adequate. She also realized her husband had made most of
the decisions, and she was frustrated trying to get a handle on managing her own household. She decided to sign on to a dating service to find someone to lean on. Three dating service contracts
later, and about $15,000 (yes, this is the dollar amount she reported
to me), she had not met Mr. Comfort and Take-Care-of-Me Man.
I was appalled that one service guaranteed sixty potential mates to
contact for $4,000. This "comfort plan" obviously made her finan-
cial status worse and dealt a serious blow to her self-esteem. This

dear widow certainly should have consulted her board of directors before taking the action she took. Her financial advisor and another godly widow would have pointed out that she was a marketing target. Her comfort level has moved lower, as has her bank account.

Another widow quickly remarried a widower, a marriage that ended in divorce a short time later. Both agreed they had remarried too soon after the death of their spouses. It has been said that we are not ready for marriage until we are at peace with who we are as an individual. This holds true for young singles, middle-aged singles, and old singles. No, we don't *feel* single, but we are. The widow who has not come to peace with who she is alone will not likely make a wise choice in either dating or choosing a mate. She will be looking for someone to take her out of "her attic," rather than a partner in her new life.

Some women remember an interest they had as a child but never pursued.

You may readily see good personal choices for comfort. Some women remember an interest they had as a child but never pursued. Now might be the time to try photography, an art class, or caring for animals. Others had no time in school years for exercise like aerobics or ballet. (Yes, older women do ballet, though maybe not wearing tights and a tutu. Tights with an overflowing cape? Maybe. This is an *appropriate* moment to say, "Who cares? Who's looking?" and leap!)

Others of us appreciate some ideas. I was asked, "What did you enjoy before you met Bob?" Being a nineteen-year-old bride who had worked on our farm, studied to get scholarships in order to go to college, and cared for our home since my mother needed to be gone, my mind was blank. We listen to others for help. Women have told me they have found comfort in:

gardening

laughing with their children

hanging out with their grandchildren (that's one of my favorites)

rediscovering the love of reading fiction

painting a room

cleaning out their closet (this does not do it for me)

water aerobics

walking and hiking

discovering a new fragrance for their living space

writing a personalized children's book for their young family members and friends

adopting a needy pet

finding household items and clothes they can donate to their favorite thrift shop

searching for a favorite new flavor of coffee or tea

Sometimes that inner comfort surprisingly overtakes us as we try something new. Sometimes it comes from doing an old familiar task, but with a different goal. We can intentionally seek it by trying new things. Sometimes we trip over it unexpectedly. Either way, dive in!

The pillar of reaching out and giving to others

In the attic we are quick learners of necessity. And learn we must, or the edges of our souls shrivel and our life becomes small. As we pass on the lessons, our resources, our story, we begin to see the reality that God accomplishes good things with bad times. We listen, especially to other widows. I have discovered that the bonds between widows have a transparency and "for real" quality that are precious. Comforting others is an essential part of our own healing.

In my attic, I learned what helped me as a caregiver. I learned to forgive "friends" who exited with Bob's exit. I learned to deal with organizations that did not have our/my best interests at heart. I learned to give up my expectations in some situations, and to articulate clearly and firmly my expectations of others. I've not graduated to the master's level in any of these areas, but I've learned something. In these past months, I have had opportunities to pass these things, and more, on to others.

I watch widows I admire and see them living the paradox of self-care, taking in comfort, and helping others, giving it out at the same time. I am assured that in my fledgling steps toward comfort, I can say with certainty:

One cannot comfort others without its sweet essence infusing one's own soul. One cannot bring joy to others without an inner smile growing so unstoppably that it breaks onto the most weary, worn face.

What do I see other widows doing to help others?

writing appropriate cards with personal words of comfort to others in need

spending more time being "Nana"

volunteering when they can for their favorite charities and ministries

starting new ministries to help those less fortunate

managing their resources in order to give to support widows in other countries

tutoring children in reading and math

tutoring young adults to pass the Graduate Equivalency Degree

The list of opportunities is endless and as diverse as each of us have been created to be. Are these worthy causes? Absolutely! Consider these examples.

Dee Brestin, a well-known author who became a widow shortly before I did, states:

> I don't particularly like being around Christians who haven't suffered deeply. They can be like Job's friends, offering pat answers, misapplying God's truths, bumping up against the knife they do not see. They smile and quote Romans 8:28 to me. I cringe. They send a card with a platitude pointing out the silver lining to my pain. I close it quickly. I know they mean well. But they plunge the knife to excruciating depths of pain. Proverbs 25:20 warns: Singing to someone in deep sorrow is like pouring vinegar in an open cut. But oh, the comfort of being with those who have truly suffered.[9]

Given our loss, we can write that card that truly comforts. We don't need to sympathize. We offer something better: our empathy. Better than feeling *for* them, we feel *with* them. My friend Joyce loves the days of the week she cares for her grandchildren. She taxis them to preschool and coordinates their activities with her son and daughter-in-law. Her calendar is now defined by the needs of her grandchildren. What a blessing! How fortunate they all are. On a recent weekend, they needed her more due to a business move and other events. When they were delivered back to their parents on Sunday night, Joyce slept for thirteen hours. What comfort in serving. What a delicious sleep!

Some of our grandparent opportunities are a short window in time. My three grandsons—two of whom are thirteen and the other twelve—may be all over the world in a mere six years. I'm honored to be their taxi now to sports, academic, and music events. In the months after Bob's exit to heaven, I realized these precious boys only knew me from the past years as Nana taking care of Grandpa. Two came to the family the same summer Bob became ill, and one had been in the family for only one year previous to this. God's timing of their adoptions is amazing. They did not know that Nana loves to laugh, play games, water ski, and other fun stuff. They knew I loved their grandpa, but knew little else about me.

I decided to change that. Besides boating, water-skiing doubles with them, and going to their activities, we've taken three road trips. We visited the battlegrounds of Chattanooga, the historic sites of Philadelphia, and the Creation Museum in Kentucky. On our Chattanooga trip we joined with my friend Jan and three of her grandchildren. What fun—and what comfort and healing to my soul! Jan had picked up that memorial stone on our "transitions" study hike in the Smokies near Gatlinburg. "Smokie Mountains 2003," she wrote on the stone. Now I have added "2006" to the stone, a reminder that good things come after transitions.

One long-distance grandma I know keeps in phone contact and prays for each family member. Some use iChat or other computer technology to see their families as they talk. Widows and widowers who have young children sense comfort from just knowing they are doing the best job they can, parenting alone. Most must lower their expectations from what they could offer when there were two parents. But I applaud their hard work to decide what priorities are a must, and letting themselves "off the hook" for the rest.

Another source for ideas is to look back to chapter 4. You completed a self-discovery tool regarding your habits, and the strengths and skills you have used in the past in jobs and volunteer projects. Whether you are seeking (and maybe needing) employment or a worthwhile place to volunteer, your discoveries can be helpful as you explore ways to experience comfort in your life. Self-care need not be exclusive from discovering a match in your current job or a new one. People with jobs or careers that don't match their skills or desires experience stress and health-related problems. There's no comfort in being locked into hours of activity in which you find little satisfaction.

Ideally, what you discovered in chapter 4 about yourself, and what you learn here about comfort can be combined to create a healthy rhythm in your new life. Being productive in a way that matches who you are is another facet of self-care.

While we'll talk more about our identity in chapter 8, it's important to mention a few aspects in this chapter. It's not unusual for a woman, upon marriage, to begin to see her identity through her relationship to her husband. The challenge for believers is to acknowledge God's design in marriage, and respect God's creation in ourselves. In God's design, when we marry, two become one. We leave our separate families and create our own. This unique, puzzling, and sometimes frustrating union must combine everything: values, lifestyles, checkbook, thermostat setting, and refrigerator contents, to name just a few challenges. Differences exist that can complement and irritate at the same time.

Before that marriage, however, God designed two unique individuals (Psalm 139). It just recently occurred to me that God *knew* before He "knit me together in my mother's womb," that I would be single again at this time. How I'm wired up from conception is adequate for today. Given the reality of marriage, we can be unaware of this truth. In the years of marriage, in our culture women are more likely to take on their husband's identity for many reasons: the priority of the male career, the culture and dynamics of role in many ethnic groups, or even some religious teachings.

> *We are not disrespecting our husband's memory to acknowledge that who we are today is different from the married woman we were.*

It is not the purpose of this book to justify, explain, or legitimize any of these. It is, however, important for the widow to examine the degree to which her identity is now locked into her husband. To the degree that our identity is linked backward to our husband, we will experience difficulty moving forward. We are not disrespecting his memory to acknowledge that who we are today is different from the married woman we were. I offer a few of my own discoveries, not because I am a good example, or even typical, but just to illustrate the point.

Bob's wife was less vocal and less direct in speech than the Miriam of today. Thankfully he influenced me toward diplomacy, gracious speech, and pausing to think before speaking. He's not here now. He cannot be hurt by Miriam's philosophies, political leanings, and musings. In my life alone, boldness is sometimes necessary. Miriam is more likely to be blunt. Bob's wife was more appreciative of a sparkling home, freshly painted inside and out, and all upkeep current. He could do it; I liked it. I can't do it; it will wait. Miriam's living space is not imploding, but, it is . . . well, different. Not so sparkly, and that's okay.

Now, for better, worse, or neutral, our other half is gone. This does not make us half a person. It simply means our new wholeness is God's creation. Yes, we have been shaped by our marriage and our mate. The impact of his life on us and the circumstances will never disappear. But in his absence, we change and our options change.

Bob knew his life calling was to serve his Lord through broadcasting at Moody Bible Institute, which is in Chicago. I did not understand "calling" and had never heard of Moody Bible Institute when I met Bob. When we married, I did not realize I was "marrying" Chicago for life. Marrying Bob was sublime; marrying Chicago was ridiculous. The icy winds that tear off Lake Michigan all winter, and the politics of this place, are not to love. The adjustment was a challenge, to be sure. And often I wished to move. But eventually I learned to love Chicago. Now, I am free to move. The choice is mine.

No matter what my future address, I'll love hot dogs smothered with everything including fresh chopped cucumbers. Never on the farm did a hot dog and cucumber reside in the same space. I'll love a real pizza, our skyline, a wind that penetrates the heaviest of coats, and all the other firsts I shared in that city with Bob.

Discovering our new identity—not apart from our spouse, but beyond him—is not a bad thing, and is often refreshing. May I encourage you to investigate this new woman? The unique woman God designed when He created you is valuable and full of potential. You and I will live and serve in worthy and good ways not in spite of our loss, but because of it. God can use our marriage and our mate, whether good, bad, or neutral, to bring about good things in our future both for ourselves and for others.

We stand on the foundation that God is Grand. We rest on the pillars of appropriate self-care and helping others in need. And in doing so we experience comfort conforming to the lumps of our life like sinking into my featherbed. Now that's real comfort.

A BIBLICAL PERSPECTIVE ON COMFORT

From the seventy-two references to *comfort* in the Old and New Testaments, we see people like us through each century seeking comfort in their times of distress. Wishing for comfort is a worthy desire, not a selfish one.

Interestingly, sometimes people visited their friend in his or her despair, and the friend refused to be comforted. (Jacob refused to be comforted by his daughter and sons when he believed his son Joseph had been killed.) Other times the friends brought more despair instead of comfort. Job, after losing his wealth and his health, as well as his children, was visited by three friends. At least they sat with him for seven days before speaking. But then they "comforted" him by telling him that he had sinned, he should repent, and his guilt deserved punishment. After Job's attempt at self-defense, they continued "comforting" him with the words that he was undermining religion, that God punishes the wicked, and that wickedness receives just retribution. (Can't you just see those words helping Job out of his attic of despair?) "Miserable comforters are you all!" Job declares in Job 16:2.

Eventually it was God answering Job's questions, bringing him understanding that brought comfort. I always like a happy ending. That was followed by God restoring his wealth and giving him more children. He held a dinner party attended by his friends and family. They comforted, consoled, and brought him silver and gold. The closest I'll get to that is the party in heaven where I'll be walking on gold! We know our attic times don't always end that way. We can be assured that we do have the option of knowing God better after our time in the attic.

The book of Psalms is a good book to read for comfort. It is full of proclamations of King David and others proclaiming that God was their comfort. Their problems were often like ours. Their friends deserted them, people took advantage of them, they saw bad people prosper and good people suffer. This was often more than annoying; they literally despaired of this life, and wanted to be in heaven instead. How did God comfort them? He did for them what He can do for us. Psalm 119 tells us

- He comforts with His promises (v. 50).
- He comforts with His laws (v. 52).
- He comforts with His love (v. 76).

There are two promises that widows especially need to lean into, in my opinion. John 3:16 is the first of these promises. This well-known verse teaches us that being a believer means this life is not the end, *and* the best is yet to come. The second promise is found in Psalm 73:17. This verse reminds us that this earth is not where all will be fair and just. Much will not make sense unless we are in His "sanctuary." In that place, we realize He is in charge of justice, not us, other people, churches, or the courts. Heaven will be fair.

God's laws are for our protection. His direction on spending and investing our resources, on relationships, on forgiveness . . . the list is endless. And they work! Disasters in our fallen world interfere. But we generally live better obeying His laws. Obedience produces comfort.

I'm so thankful that His love is "new every morning" (Lamentations 3:23). I need a different love today than yesterday. Yesterday I needed to know His love would adequately replace Bob's love. Today with my grandson Edmond in surgery at this moment, I need to know that His love is so great for Edmond that He will bring him through, that wholeness and strength will prevail in his young body. Being loved is the greatest human need. We are promised that love from our Creator (Isaiah 54:5; Jeremiah 31:3; Hosea 2:19–20).

This chapter can only touch the surface of what God tells us about comfort in His Word. Study on! Here are more references on comfort for starters.

- ◆ Comfort is the antidote for excessive sorrow (2 Corinthians 2:7).
- ◆ Comfort after sorrow produces patient endurance (2 Corinthians 1:6).
- ◆ Comfort is the blessing promised to those who mourn (Matthew 5:4).

Your time before an open Bible will, in and of itself, bring comfort. My wish for you is that you seek it, it finds you, and you pass it on.

Section Three

RELATIONSHIPS:
NEVER THE SAME

Chapter Six

FRIENDS:

Letting Go and
Loving the Real Thing

———— ∞∞ ————

"The friend who holds your hand and says the wrong thing
is made of dearer stuff than the one who stays away."
—BARBARA KINGSOLVER

I had read that widows report losing 75 percent of the people they
believed were their friends. *That won't be me*, I thought, as
friends flooded our lives during my husband's terminal illness.

But I found that this statistic *has* been true for me as well. A
well-known Christian author, upon becoming a widower, was no
longer spoken to at his Sunday school class—a class that he and his
wife had been attending for years. Having his arrivals and departures enveloped in silence was too painful, and he stopped going. I
understand. Gender is irrelevant here; the pain remains. Once we've
heard all the "reasons" for people dropping out of our lives, the
truth must be faced. Behavior does not lie. Not all people in our
lives before were our true friends. Of course, some were and still
are, but everything has changed.

For those of you reading this book to gain understanding of
our experience, can I be real? Here are some reasons I heard from
people who were no longer part of my circle of friends:

"We thought you needed space."

50 percent of my world is gone. I'd say there's a little extra space here.

Space for what?

"After a year or two, will you return to pick up our friendship?"

I'm sure I'll be a different person by then.

"Everyone is so busy."

Our calendars simply reveal our priorities.

"They don't know what to say."

It's hard for me to let adults off the hook with that one.

Silent presence is better than absence.

Showing up and saying, **"I don't know what to say,"** might be better than silence.

It's impossible for me to let Christ-followers off the hook with that one. When we claim as our Lord the God of all comfort, we can show up and trust that His wisdom will instruct us.

This next one requires a little more examination, and I hesitate to put it in print; however, we're being real here, right? Yes, I've heard this as a possible explanation. "You are now a threat to other women in that group because you are single." Does this person realize that what she is saying is that her husband is only faithful because there are no other single, available women around? That's an insult to the quality of the marriage and the integrity of the husband. There's also an implication about my standards as well.

"Aha, you too?
I thought I was alone
—until now."

In the months that I have been alone, I have come to chuckle over much of what I see and hear. I have also had the opportunity to help educate some of these dear people as they truly do mean well. I have learned much myself and look back at some of *my* behavior in the past. I wish I could do a rewind of some of my own blunders.

MYTHS ABOUT FRIENDSHIP

May I share with you some of the myths we widows believe? This list has evolved as I have become friends with a growing circle of widows who have been willing to be transparent with me. Our bond of widowhood, which, of course, we do not want, nor would we choose, is nevertheless a powerful bond. We find ourselves describing an event in our lives or a feeling, and our new friend communicates, "Aha, you too? I thought I was alone—until now." Our circle of friends and acquaintances also believe many of these myths, making it difficult (this is an understatement) to move into our new life without our mate. We'll look at these myths: friends understand what you are experiencing, friendship from the past predicts friendship in the future, all types of friends have your best interests at heart, and quantity is better than quality.

MYTH # 1: *Friends understand what you are experiencing.*

Unless a person has lost her/his spouse through death she/he does not understand what is happening to those of us who have. People do, with kindly intentions, refer to important losses in *their* lives. I have had people refer to the loss of a grandparent, a beloved parent, a dear friend, a brother or sister. I listen and nod my head. I hope they don't talk long. Do they crawl into an empty cold bed at night? Do they reach in the grocery freezer to pick up potpies and realize there is no one pulling in the driveway who loves potpies? Do they stare in the refrigerator and realize they don't even know the kind of food *they* like? Do they run their fingers through their hair and realize theirs will be the only fingers making that simple, sweet gesture?

Of course, it is unfair for us to expect them to understand. If we set up an impossible expectation, then we *will* be disappointed. While a divorcée has gone through some of the same aspects of loss, there are significant differences as well. In talking with my divorced friends, I hear that theirs is a different kind of anger. Many divorcées also feel rejection added to their sense of loss. The impact of divorce on a woman's self-esteem is different, though both widows and divorcées usually suffer feelings of lower self-worth.

What is my response to these well-meaning friends? I am grateful they are trying. I try to have an "exit" statement in my mind in case I can listen no more. *And* I'm writing this book!

MYTH # 2: *Friendship from the past predicts friendship in the future.*

We have said earlier that marriage creates a strange and paradoxical entity. Two become one. What a mystery. Couple friendships are usually based on who you were with your husband—in my case, Team Neff, Bob and Miriam. Our topics of conversation, our travels, our humor, the music we listened to, and much more, were Team Neff. And now 50 percent of Team Neff is gone. Fifty percent of *me* is gone as well. Silly me. It was immature thinking on my part to believe that our past friendships would remain the same as they'd been. My universe has changed. So must everything in it.

I have often stated I was a better woman because of Bob. A man of gracious speech, patient listening, an "other-oriented" person, he made me better than I am. Who am I without that? The package here has changed, and I have come to peace with the fact that some friendships of the past are no longer in the "good match" category. Rediscovering my love of galloping, loosening the reins, leaning forward, and watching my horse's hooves gobble up the beach is not everyone's cup of tea. Sailing alone on a catamaran, sail, rudder, and only the wind at my back on the ocean is not the Miriam they knew before. (I did not know that Miriam either!)

My children say I am more blunt now, and I rather believe they are correct. I remember during my husband's intense and long battle with ALS that I spoke often with our support group social worker about all the "stuff" in my life: the endless necessity of relentlessly pursuing insurance claims, disability disputes, and much more. I felt I had to become a battle-ax to secure the appropriate necessities, treatment, and the best care for Bob. "Will I return to 'nice' again after this is all over?" I asked our social worker, Laurie, who had also become my friend. "No," was her soft but true answer. "When you discover what you have about companies, people, life, and death, you are never the same." I appreciated her candor. Wishing to be the exception did not make it true. The friends from the past would discover a new person if they stayed in the friendship.

Why are we frustrated admitting that the way a relationship has been in the past is not how it will remain in the future? Because before, we got to choose our friendships. We felt changes coming and intentionally moved away from, or closer to, others. We chose. Becoming a widow was not our choice. The exodus simply happens. We are left puzzling over whether we said or did something wrong. No, my dear friend. The team is gone. But the new you will attract some new people and new opportunities as well.

MYTH # 3: *All types of friends have your best interests at heart.*

There are at least three different words in Scripture that are all translated into the English word *friend*.

1. *Philos* (noun) one who loves, as in Proverbs 17:9, 18:24
2. *Hetairos* (noun) a comrade/companion/partner, as in Proverbs 18:24
3. *Peitho* (verb) to persuade, influence, as in Proverbs 14:20 (one who uses another for their interests)[10]

Our *philos* friends love us. They are willing to swallow our less-than-perfect behavior and protect our reputation. They love us unselfishly, without an agenda, and they just keep showing up. I am humbled and undeserving of the way some of my friends have stepped into my world, into the shattered mess of my grieving, and found ways to bring laughter. They find a way to make us look good when we don't care.

May I digress with a personal example? I had friends who literally took it upon themselves to make me look good when I did not care. Due to the nature of my husband's illness, amyotrophic lateral sclerosis, a three-year period of my life moved into a cloud with only one goal—to walk beside my husband through his valley and bring to his life as much quality, peace, and joy as I could. Taking care of myself was not on the "to-do" list.

In timing that I yet do not understand, he exited this world for heaven three months before my contractual, scheduled retirement after twenty-six years counseling in public high schools. By contract, I needed to return to work five days after his celebration/funeral. Needless to say, one very numb person made her way into her office and went through the motions of her last months of work. To my dismay, there were numerous retirement events that I needed to show up for. I knew if I did not make an effort to be there that I would later regret missing these occasions. Now this may sound quite trivial to you, but I had nothing to wear, and it kind of mattered. My size had changed, larger, of course, and everything I owned was old. My tenacious couple friends Steve and Carol met me at a restaurant (that in and of itself was a treat) with two large Chico boxes in the booth. Can you imagine friends who *give* you a total outfit with various tops that make you look good? Can you imagine a flattering jacket covered with parrots? How could I help but smile in my new clothes? Let me tell you, the pictures of me at the functions with my friends and family are the best rendition of me that was possible, given the circumstances. Now, beyond real is the fact that they also added to my ensemble at Christmas. I had something for every occasion because of my *philos*—ones who love—friends.

Our *hetairos* friends are partners on the same mission as we are. If we continue to care about the same things we did when we were a couple, these friends persist. Often, those causes are no longer so important to us. They may have featured an interest our husband had (e.g., golfing). They may have been mission projects that were more his heartbeat than ours. In some cases, those causes may still be very important to us, but not always. Usually business associates fall into this category. But if the shared career interest disappears, those *hetairos* friends usually do too.

I heard of one widow who continued to give generously to every project she and her husband had supported. She got into financial difficulties and was unable to pay her own bills. Unwilling to admit that her resources had dwindled, she continued. Upon her death, her finances were a mess. Of course, her favored charities were not responsible for cleaning up the mess; her children were. God didn't get glory for that.

I am told by widows who have been on the journey much longer than I that all will be well. I am already beginning to imagine that. A friend from school invited me to join her on a hiking trip in Maine in the fall of my first year alone. Of the ten hikers, I knew only her, and fully expected to enjoy this new possibility of friendships. Indeed, that happened. I loved these new, adventurous, spirited, positive women and continue to enjoy new friendships because of the times we spent in Acadia, Maine.

Our *peitho* friends are really not friends. They are users. One example of this is people who have a financial plan for your life. If you sense someone has become your friend in order to sell you something, go back to chapter 3 and review how to make financial decisions. While you do need input from wise people, and you can consult your board of directors, those bottom-line decisions are yours. Remember, salespersons are salespersons. Their motivation is to sell you something. They are more likely to sell you something if you believe you have something in common with them. They ask you questions to "get to know you better." They want you to *feel* that they are your friends.

I am told that some widows are pursued by men who perhaps have lost their spouse as well. While many wonderful marriages result from this scenario, it must be acknowledged that some men are mostly looking for another caregiver or a supplemental paycheck. Your board of directors will help you discern the motivations of the new people in your life. For those of us who are visual, here's a simple exercise that helps us understand changes in our friendships.

Our Friendship Mobile

Can you picture a mobile with its delicately balanced pieces fluttering in the breeze? This represents our friendships in our married life. Your friendship mobile might look something like this:

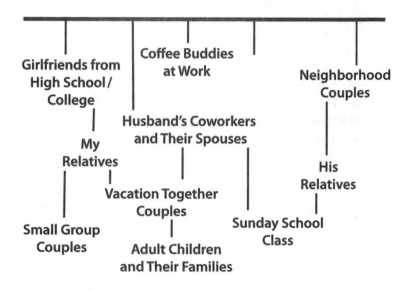

Take a few minutes and draw your friendship mobile from your married life. Highlight the pieces that were especially important to you. If a white board is available use that. When I first taught this concept in a class for widows, having drawn the mobile on the board, I handed an eraser to one of the widows.

"What happened when your husband died?" I asked. She began to erase chunks of her previous mobile. In her case she had to take her husband's business partner to court. What she thought was a trusting friendship, including shared vacations, turned out to be anything but that. While different widows erase different parts, the exercise helped all of us understand the realities of the changes we were experiencing.

I gained perspective to my own situation by asking myself these questions:

- Why were they in my mobile to begin with?
- Why should they remain from my perspective?
- Why should they remain from their perspective?
- What mutual benefit is to be gained by them in a continued friendship?
- What mutual benefit is to be gained by me in a continued friendship?

I was unable to even think of asking myself these questions for at least eight months into my solitary life. The answers, somewhere between uncomfortable and painful, at least explained why my mobile had changed. It also highlighted that many of our friendships had been *hetairos*, those of comrades on a shared mission, as opposed to *philos*, one who loves me.

Wouldn't you rather see the truth and move on? I found freedom to release people in my previous mobile (they had exited anyway). I found freedom to face forward rather than trying to figure out what happened. I found freedom to begin the search for what mattered to me. This freedom lightens your checkbook obligations, clears your calendar, and is quite refreshing.

Since we are being real here, perhaps one last topic should be addressed. It is tempting to categorize past friendships as superficial (those that don't exist anymore) and real (those who remain). Examining reality, it is possible and probably likely that some of the perceived couple friendships we experienced existed because a coworker did truly care deeply about our mate. However, their connection with us was secondary and convenient. We know that behavior never lies. Admitting this, while painful, is necessary in order to heal from that hurt and move forward.

Have you finished erasing from your mobile? Perhaps the size of the "his relatives" piece has now shrunk. Redrawing our mobile and adjusting it to the realities of today frees us to create new pieces or enlarge small pieces from our past. Our new mobile will not be empty, though at times it feels that way. But it will be different. For example, girlfriends from your job may become your new travel buddies. Friends from school days may become important again.

As I was contemplating what had happened to my friendship mobile, I recalled a chunk of Scripture, John 6. In this chapter Jesus experiences a huge reversal in popularity. While I had studied this in the past, Jesus' experience and words took on new meaning in this season of my life. Jesus had been gaining in popularity as word of His healing of people spread. Can you imagine what buzz that would create, given the medical expertise of that time? The crowd that followed Him at that time is stated to have been five thousand people. However, some scholars surmise that counting at that time only included males. If this were the case the crowd may have been twelve thousand when women and children were added in. We can leave that to the theologians to debate. But either way, we're talking big numbers here. (We might call it a megachurch meeting.)

Briefly, the biblical account tells us that Jesus took a boy's lunch of five loaves and two fish. He instructed the disciples to have the people sit down, and, with this small amount of food, performed a miracle and fed everyone. Besides Jesus' ability to miraculously provide food for thousands of people, there is another important lesson to be discovered. The next day the crowds were following their leads to find Jesus. When they found Him, they began a serious dialogue about more than food. Some wanted more miracles as proof He was the Messiah. Some were set on proving He was an imposter. Some trusted Him to be who He said He was.

Jesus exposed the real Jesus. He told them who He was. "When many of his disciples heard it, they said, "This teaching is difficult; who can accept it?" (John 6:60 NRSV) The group of followers might have been around seventy at that time. This included his inner group of twelve as well as other committed followers, including women and seekers who were willing to accept Him for who He was, as well as some skeptics. By verse 66 the group has shrunk again. "Because of this many of his disciples turned back and no longer went about with him"(NRSV). Had these disciples seen Him do good things? Had these disciples even possibly helped hand out miracle food and collect miracle leftovers? Had these disciples known His background? Had these disciples heard Him explain who He was and what He was about? Yes, yes, yes, and yes. Now we can see the masses separating into the three types of "friends" we looked at earlier: the users, the buddies or comrades, and the remaining *philo* friends. "So Jesus asked the twelve, 'Do you also wish to go away?'" (John 6:67 NRSV)

As I studied, I gained insight into the nature of our connections with other people. I also recognized anew that, in fact, Jesus has experienced everything we have in our human losses. He understands. Changing circumstances certainly changes our mobile. I gained a fresh perspective of talking to Jesus about the voids in my life. There is truly nothing I experience that He has not already experienced. The people who remained with Jesus came to know and accept who He really was, rather than the person they hoped Him to be. Perhaps there will be an element of that truth in our changing mobile. After contemplating Jesus' experience, I think we can add another myth about friendships to our list.

MYTH # 4: *Quantity is better than quality.*

While quantity is certainly valued in our culture for most aspects of people's lives, it should not be true when it comes to friendships. It's hard not to get caught up in the quantity notion when we think of the messages bombarding our minds daily. The old message from our adolescence is that the cool person is the popular one with lots of friends. They get voted into office, made queen of this, and president of that. The person of few friends is, well, the wallflower, somehow less worthy than the popular girl.

Having many handbags, shoes, shirts, or any product is better than having just a few—and if you buy a look-alike of the real thing for less money, you can have ten of them! I love the idea of a bargain, but some folks get swept into overspending in order to have a quantity of everything. I was especially aware of this in the last decade of my counseling in our public high school. I saw girls in my office whose wardrobe costs kept them from spending money on college applications. And they had a different look every day. Which has the greatest potential for future returns? The "quantity now" message is powerful.

We as widows are especially vulnerable to the quantity myth because of our loneliness. I understand. When I think about my past life of talking with and interacting with people all day in my work as a high school counselor—added to life with my husband, which meant participating with Bob on social events connected with the boards he sat on, his extensive network of coworkers, our personal friends, and most significantly, his presence in my life 24/7 as my best friend—well, this new life seems unreal. These days in retirement and widowhood are quiet beyond belief. I treasure more than ever my precious handful of friends. However, I also enjoy solitude.

Not all widows do. Be careful if you are one of those more intense people persons. You are more vulnerable to connecting with people for quantity's sake, not quality. Then you are more likely to be dipping into the "comrades" group. This is okay if you share a common mission. But you may also dip into the "user" group. This will eventually bring disaster. Being desperate for companionship creates a blindness to the user aspect of new relationships. Friends and family often recognize users before widows do. Disaster is a sure thing; the only aspect in question is, will the disaster happen sooner or later?

Let me illustrate from my family tree. (I am not proud of this.) My mother died at age seventy-five. While my three sisters and I knew our dad to be a people person, we thought that since he was seventy-nine and had been married to our mother for forty-nine years, he would remain single. Living in the small town in the area they had called home since their marriage, it seemed likely he would be content with the friendships he had.

Wrong. We learned after the fact that our dad had remarried. We had never heard of this person he had married, and were upset by the surprise. We accepted the reality, however, and determined that if this was good for him, we were okay with it. Do you know how many secrets there are in small towns? Not many in the summertime when windows are open, and when everyone talks at the local coffee shop. We knew from our dad's complaints to us, as well as to others, who felt it their duty to keep us informed, that there were plenty of arguments in the new marriage. We also knew that money was being spent for things of little interest or value to our dad. Eventually, as divorce loomed, my dad was told what, to him, was the final insult. His new wife informed him that she had only married him for his dental insurance! Post-divorce, he was once again lonely, as well as poorer, but this time wiser.

We need to become good people pickers.

How can we choose what friendships to cultivate from those remaining in our mobile? How can we find new people with whom to cultivate mutually enriching relationships? How can we avoid the users without painful blunders to discover who they really are? We need to become good people pickers. Before we embarked on this solitary life, we had some skills at picking people in our lives. Most choices were so determined by our circumstances and our mate that those skills might be inadequate for our new life today. Again, for those of us who are visual, I've developed a little chart that we can use in picking people for our new life.

Years of living in the adult world teaches us that people differ in character. However, it takes more than years of living to discern character. We are looking for a few good friendships. I have found that the book of all wisdom, the Bible, is an excellent resource for defining and describing character. The continuum on my chart goes from the person we want to avoid—a fool—to a person we would wish as a friend—a wise person.

By way of explanation, we do not define a person as a fool. Her behavior defines her as such. Likewise, a wise person's behavior defines her as such. We are not labeling the person, we are just examining the behavior. ("By their fruit you will know them.") Author Jan Silvious wrote the excellent book *Fool-Proofing Your Life*.[11] I am indebted to her for her practical thoughts on the impact fools have on us, and received her permission to elaborate on the concept. *Caution*: Just because we pick someone does not mean that will result in a growing friendship. A two-way relationship cannot be created by one person. But we can decide where we want to invest our emotional energy by giving some thought to this chart.

FACTS ABOUT FOOLS	FACTS ABOUT WISE WOMEN
Fools exist.	Wise women exist.
We don't identify fools. Matthew 5:21–23	Any woman can become a wise woman. Proverbs 2:1–11
Fools identify themselves. Proverbs 12:23	Wise women identify themselves by their actions. Proverbs 3:13–18
God identifies fools. Proverbs 1:7	God identifies wise women. Proverbs 3:13–18
A fool will not be reconciled. Proverbs 20:3, 29:9	A wise woman seeks reconciliation. Proverbs 19:11; Romans 12:18
A fool is always right. Proverbs 12:15	A wise woman knows she is imperfect. Proverbs 2:1–5, 20:9
A fool trusts herself. Proverbs 1:32, 28:26	A wise woman trusts God, not herself. Proverbs 2:6–11
A fool doesn't think straight. Proverbs 18:2, 22:3	A wise woman thinks straight. Romans 12:1–3
A fool repeats her folly. Proverbs 26:11, 27:12	A wise woman learns from her failure. Psalm 119:65–68
A fool reveals only her own mind. Proverbs 18:2	A wise woman seeks God's mind. Psalm 119:45–48
A fool does not listen. Proverbs 1:22–32	A wise woman listens. Proverbs 1:33
A fool does not think. Proverbs 14:16	A wise woman thinks. Proverbs 4:26–27
A fool does not learn. Proverbs 17:10	A wise woman learns. Psalm 119:105, 124–125
A fool believes there is no God. Psalm 53:1	A wise woman knows God IS and guides. Psalm 121:1–4
A fool wrecks herself/blames God. Proverbs 19:3	A wise woman accepts responsibility. Proverbs 19:21; Romans 14:12

As we spend time with a person, we can ask ourselves questions about the person's behavior in each of these eleven areas.

Some are easy to answer from just talking and hanging out. Others take a little more time, perception, and observation.

- Is she/he "at odds" with many people from her past, as well as her present?
- Does she/he communicate "my way or the highway"?
- Does her/his behavior reflect biblical instruction and guidance?
- Does she/he have the uncommon quality of common sense?
- Does she/he repeat unhealthy patterns and unwise choices (i.e., stays in debt, stays in destructive relationships, repeatedly lacks self-care)?
- Is she/he self-absorbed? Does she strive to monopolize your calendar?
- Does she/he monopolize conversations? Does she selectively listen to others, including you?
- Do you find yourself doing mental gymnastics trying to understand her/his statements, reasoning, or beliefs?
- Does she/he seem to get stuck in unwise situations and relationships either with an inability to see what's real or the unwillingness to act on what's real?
- Does her/his speech and behavior mirror her belief in God and desire to humbly attempt to live likewise?
- Are her/his problems always someone else's fault, including God's?

How can we tell we are vulnerable to becoming involved in friendships not in our best interests? When we *excuse behavior* in the foolish category, we are vulnerable. When we accept/tolerate behavior not in our best interests, we are vulnerable. Often, before we recognize the behavior, we sense an uncomfortable feeling. Do you feel emotionally and even physically drained just being around a person? That is a warning flag. Do you find yourself rationalizing his/her behavior? "She/he says . . ." and refers to future behavior that will be different from what you are seeing now.

For example:

◆ "I'll be paying off that maxed credit card when I get my raise in three months."

◆ "I'll be able to call you more often when this work project is done."

Remember, behavior never lies. "He/she does that because . . . ," and you rationalize poor behavior by past circumstances.

◆ "I'm partly to blame because . . . ," and you accept poor behavior of another person because of your poor behavior.

Solution to the "I'm partly to blame syndrome":

◆ Straighten up your act, girlfriend, and see if his or hers changes! OR

◆ Don't inappropriately accept blame to help someone else look better.

Does this process seem hard at times? Does it require more focused attention than you feel you have? Becoming a good people picker is not easy. If you wonder if it's worth the effort, talk to a widow who invested time in a new friendship that proved to be controlling and then ended badly. My friend experienced this; in her loneliness she let her new friend plan some vacations and become involved with her family. As their "friendship" developed, my friend's calendar was consumed with another person's wishes and agenda. Becoming strong enough to say "No, thanks" was hard, and the ending of the relationship rocky. It's better to invest the energy upfront and avoid the painful ending.

MOVING ON

The personal work of examining our mobile hasn't been easy, has it? While we are grieving the loss of our mate, we also grieve the loss of our friends. They seem so insignificant compared to the huge loss of our husband. In a sense, however, it's like the last straw because losing them was unexpected. *And* they're still around. Yes, our paths do cross sometimes, and we start to feel the pain of the old wound. However, we have some new wisdom to lean into. We know that the real friends, the ones who loved us, are still our friends. We know that the friends who have exited were our comrades or users, not our *philos* friends. We have not lost those treasures.

In discovering the true nature of the "friends" who have left, it is normal to feel bitter and/or angry and/or betrayed. In our anguish of feeling bitter, angry, and betrayed, we are in the perfect spot for God to do one of the works He most specializes in: forgiveness. Forgiveness is the single most important thing we can do to move on. Learning about the three kinds of friends and being real was a great help to me in forgiving. I recognized that we are all humanoids—my word for ordinary people with clay feet. I am one myself, though my "clayness" sometimes creeps upward. There were many other humanoids in my original mobile. We're letting go of a comrade or buddy, not a dear friend. We're letting go of someone with whom we shared an interest, not a dear friend. Forgiveness frees us to let go. The void is no longer painful but rather an available space for either new people or new projects and adventures. And, as surely as the sun sets in the evening and rises bringing a new day, those will come.

I hiked beneath the snow-laden pines of woods where deer had hunkered down the night before. The indentations in the snow marked their presence. The evergreen scent was pungent and exhilarating. Carol, our hiking leader, came beside me to get better acquainted. She seemed to know every type of evergreen we passed and what kind of bird was creating each song. *Aha, another woman who loves the out-of-doors,* I thought. An athletic, effervescent individual, and one who had triumphed over cancer, she seemed intimate with nature. *This is a person I wish to know better.* We talk. I'm thankful for my new hiking hobby.

As I pored over the manual she assembled about our hike in Acadia, Maine, a sense of anticipation crept into my spirit, a feeling I had not felt for four years. It felt good. I could check off whale watching or sea kayaking under the activities I was interested in pursuing. I opted for whale watching because I had already experienced sea kayaking. I sensed these fellow hikers might be an interesting part of my new friendship mobile. I was right.

I pause to reflect. I'm caught off guard by my awareness of the richness of this new life. I never wished for it; I never dreamed it would be so different. But I'm facing forward with new opportunities for friendship. Smells like hope to me.

Chapter Seven

FAMILY:

Healing after
the Tree Shakes

—∞∞∞—

"I like trees because they seem more resigned to the
way they have to live than other things do."
—WILLA CATHER

Warmth, comfort, connection, stories, history, context: our families bring all this and more to our lives. Surprises, heartbreak, adventure, even shock and awe: families can bring all this as well. What happens with this new loss we experience? I can promise you one thing. Change, change, and more change. Will the surprises ever end? Will anything in our world become predictable again? Yes, in time there will be a new rhythm in our life. Our new friendship network will emerge. Our finances will stabilize. Our emotional roller coaster will become a more fluid carriage ride. All these things take place, for better or worse, in the context of family.

Whether small or large, rejecting or supportive, absent or present, most of us have at least some adventures with family after we become (*ugh*, there's that word again) widows. Family relationships change when we lose our husbands. This is reality. We would be naïve not to expect that children, cousins, grandparents, brothers, and sisters will not be affected by our mutual loss. This change becomes messy because we all make assumptions about each other's feelings. And often we are wrong.

CHANGES WILL COME

In my experience, there were surprising changes in our family, both positive and sad, after Bob's final departure. Positive changes included:

- Being able to devote time and energy to being Nana to my grandchildren
- More flexibility of schedule to connect with family, accommodating their schedules
- More empathy for widows in our family and others who have suffered great losses
- A new one-on-one relationship with each of my adult children

Not all is positive, however, as you already well know. I was saddened by the different look in my children's eyes when they entered my home after the loss of their father. I see and hear about ways they are trying to stay connected to their memories of him. I share some here, not because your children will do the same things, but rather to illustrate that children are different. Recognizing their differences is a gift we give them, offering them permission to grieve in their own way.

Bob was a car washer, no, a car *detailer*. He taught each of his children how to wash a car so that every part sparkled. (Why do tires matter? They are supposed to be dirty, aren't they?) He did it by example. They worked beside him. Rather than instruct them on how to wash a car, they spoke of other things as they worked. Shortly after his departure, one son came home and spent six hours washing and detailing his car. That was not surprising. But the next day he returned and did the same thing again! "Rob, I thought you did that yesterday." The look in my eyes communicated to him that I was trying to understand what was going on. "It's how I connect with Dad. He's with me when I'm washing my car." His usually easy, charming grin was too stiff. I knew it did not match the feelings in his heart. He was trying to be strong for his mom. And he was missing his dad. I sensed that his car would be sparkling for a long time.

Of course, I cried that night for my son. I cried for his loss. I cried for his yearning for his dad. I cried for the gazillion ways Bob's namesake would miss his dad.

Another son just took his dad's car out for a drive, a long drive. "It was as if I was giving Dad a ride somewhere. I felt him with me." That made so much sense, as son John often drove his dad to work after ALS immobilized his arms and his legs. In those months, John saw more of the real character of a good dad. And that good dad's presence still rides with him in that car. My daughter chooses to put her dad's kind of music on in the car when she is driving alone to her legal internship. Classical, operatic, great traditional hymns; he sang them well, and so does she—full volume!

I was saddened to see some relatives remove Bob's picture from their homes. I can forgive them, because I know they just cannot, at this time, handle the painful reminder of the person they lost. Other widows have seen this in their families. We understand, but we don't want our husbands to be forgotten. The exception would be—and I've spoken to widows who have had this experience— when their husband was simply a negative in their life and the lives of the extended family. Another I have observed is when that person's pain needs a season of denial before moving forward. I trust we do not judge each other. Their necessity of this denial season is survival for them. Remember, we said in chapter 1 that our grieving is so different. So is that of our relatives.

One friend attended a holiday gathering in another state after her husband's death. "Oh, I miss Sam so much," a cousin, aunt, or uncle would say. They saw him, at most, once a year. No one empathized with my friend and the enormity of *her* loss. In fact, no one asked her how she was doing! While she was still numb, she was not so numb that she couldn't hurt more. Not one of them acknowledged that they understood that her loss as his wife was the greatest. She was able on her lengthy ride home to forgive them. And she also decided she would not make that trip again, at least not for a very long time. Her decision to spend Christmases in other ways was wise on her part, at least for now.

Your relatives' loss is not the same as yours. They cannot

understand your 24/7 emptiness. Even if they tell you they understand, remember, they cannot. This recognition gives us freedom to forgive and overlook comments we hear. It's not unusual for some family relationships to be temporarily or even permanently severed by the trauma of losing a very important person. In my conversations with many widows, some were blamed for their husband's death. One young widow with no children was blamed by his parents for allowing him to be a firefighter. He lost his life in the line of duty, in a profession he had chosen and loved. This widow joined our group because she felt so utterly alone. We were able to comfort her and reassure her that their assessment might change. Remember, initial reactions may not be permanent. We gave her permission to create space between her and his relatives so she could heal. Temporary? Permanent? Time will tell.

Being an educator and a "list" person, I attempted to make sense of our family changes visually. Here's a simple exercise that helped me understand. I drew my family tree on a whiteboard. It looked something like this:

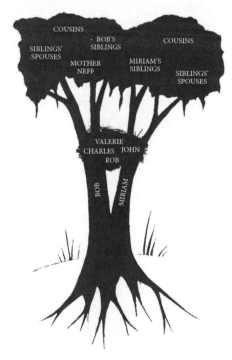

These were the people surrounding Bob and me and our four children. While there are others, they were not regularly in our lives. When you draw your family tree, it may look quite different. Some have immediate family, who for all practical purposes, have already left the family tree. Erase the branch of your husband. I know this is painful. Please know it can help in our healing and understanding even though this is a tough, tough, exercise.

When I removed Bob's branch, it helped me see why every other connection became fragile and less predictable. Even though I had, and continue to have, good relationships with Bob's side of the family, Bob was the primary connecting person. Without him we must create a new and different relationship. What will that be? I don't know. We're still in process.

I've discovered that hearing others' stories helps me sort out my own.

I've discovered that hearing others' stories helps me sort out my own. One woman went to a wedding shortly after her loss and was seated with couples at the reception. Family she was closest to were seated at other tables. In her new, fragile state, this did not work. Everyone knew of her husband's death, but no word of acknowledgment was spoken. After a one-sided "conversation" of listening to one individual expound on irrelevant trivia with no acknowledgment of her husband's absence, she made her exit. She escaped to the quiet haven of her home, preferring comforting memories to pretending to be interested in a monologue.

Our mate's absence is so glaringly evident at family events. Some may not mention him unless you do. If you are reading this hoping to better understand your widow friend/relative, I recommend that you *do* refer to him. Your grieving relative is quite aware of her husband's absence and the difference it would make if he were there. To speak of him assures her that he was important to you too. She does not want him to be forgotten, and silence implies that is happening.

After doing our exercise with the whiteboard and our family tree, we see with our today eyes that "family" will never be the same. Accepting that fact is a huge step toward healing and moving forward. As long as we grasp the past, we are not free to establish new bonds and look for fresh ways to relate to each person in the family tree. This time of transition can be like the Grand Pause in a symphony.

As a French horn player, I loved the grand and moving symphonies. Composers interjected a Grand Pause in their compositions to give emphasis to a crescendo, as well as to anticipate a change in the mood for the next movement. The Grand Pause was a moment to take a deep breath, let the emotion of the last movement sweep over and through your senses, and anticipate a new melody, harmony, or rhythm. The pause was, well, grand.

This modification of our family is a good time for reflection, time for a Grand Pause. If possible, step back and try to take an objective look at your family tree. It helps in being objective if you think of the individuals not as relatives, but as friends. You might even determine which of the three types of friends they would be, based on our chapter on friendships.

Before, were they people who loved you for who you were? Will they be friends who love the new you for who you are? Not necessarily. Remember, you are different; you're not the person they knew before.

Before, was your connection based on a common bond? What was the common bond? If it is gone, will there be an enduring relationship? Adult children sometimes discover after the death of both parents that there seems to be little left in terms of a common bond. Siblings must discover whether their relationship as siblings merits staying connected. The same holds true when your mate is no longer here for connection. Is there a surviving bond to maintain connection? Before, were they users? This is a bold question to ask, and some would prefer to pretend rather than face that reality. But pretending may set you up for more hurt, especially if you must pay some price to keep the connection with users. To be blunt, they are in your life because you have something they can use for their personal well-being. Are you willing to "pay to play"?

Early in the chapter, we said that we can make wrong assumptions about relatives' feelings at this time. It is a wise policy in the early weeks and months to let time sort out behavior. We may assume the worst because we are grieving and our whole world looks grey. Checking in with our board of directors for feedback may prevent us from confronting members of the extended family when everyone's nerves are stretched.

Typical stress points include:

- ◆ Differences in care and attention through illness
- ◆ Interest in financial matters above emotional support
- ◆ Differences in how to publicly acknowledge, memorialize, or celebrate the event
- ◆ Blame, especially if death was unexpected and unexplainable
- ◆ Blame, if death was due to suicide
- ◆ Past issues with loss that surface unexpectedly
- ◆ Rivalry or competition unresolved from the past

You may be unaware of unresolved issues that relatives had with your husband.

This list could be endless, but I think you get the point. At this time, a hurricane of problems can appear from nowhere and create more damage to the already-fragile family tree. You may be unaware of unresolved issues that relatives had with your husband. In fact, he may have been unaware of those as well. His exit exposes those feelings, and with new intensity the tree shakes again. You are left wondering why. Like an iceberg with most of its cold, blue hardness unexposed, but nevertheless real and lethal, the exit of your husband reveals truths about the family tree you did not recognize before. You may never know or understand some of the behavior of the birds in your family tree, especially in those early months.

This is why I recommend a Grand Pause, if possible, to let time sort out behavior. Who will continue to be in your life? At what level? Peripheral? Central? Remember, behavior does not lie. The mist of words will float away; actions will do the talking. After the Grand Pause for reflection, I have found that some family bonds have become stronger and have a new depth of meaning. This is a precious discovery in the aftermath of the family tree shake-up.

PARENTING ALONE: A SPECIAL WORD ABOUT CHILDREN AT HOME

The loss of their father has a great impact on children who are in their formative years. Because of this, I want to devote a section on families to children from birth to age eighteen. While my children were older when Bob died, I have many widowed friends (and widowers too) with young children who have been transparent with me. Also in my twenty-six years as a high school counselor, I was professionally involved with students who lost a parent through death. It is important that we try to understand their experience, and explore resources available to help them through this ordeal.

I have chosen to do this by sharing real life struggles of widows and widowers who have contacted me through Widowconnection .com. With their permission, and by changing details to protect their privacy, I share their story.

Please see appendix A on page 183 for a special word about children at home.

NEXT STEPS: YOUR NEW RELATIONSHIPS

Just when you think the family tree is finally settling after the severe shake-up, another wind may be on the way. How will family members respond when there are new people in your life? Little notice, positive or negative, will be taken if new friends are women if you are a widow, or men if you are a widower. These new friendships do happen as we take up new hobbies, join new groups, travel, exercise, or whatever other new interests come our way.

The picture is quite different, especially if the new person is a potential mate. I could fill pages here with sweet stories of new marriages of both young widows and vintage widows. We would all smile, sigh, and wish them "happily ever after—again!" Not all new relationships have that happy ending. Good books have been written, such as Mary Whelchel's *Common Mistakes Singles Make and How to Avoid Them,* [12] on evaluating new relationships and dating. I recommend reading this book and others if you know you want to remarry. Those principles apply to us even though we may not like the label "single." There are a few important things to mention here that specifically relate to widows and new relationships.

Widows are vulnerable. Divorcées and other single women may be vulnerable as well. But our situation is a bit different. For those who want to remarry, they wish to be loved and valued for who they are. They may be perceived, however, as potential caregivers, financial security, or someone to fill emptiness. When these are the predominate reasons for marriage, unhappiness is on the way.

Children matter. Children may or may not relate well to Mom's or Dad's remarriage. Children typically do not like surprises. They do like to be included in the discussions of how you are feeling, and what you are looking for in a new relationship. Of course, they do not have the final word. But they can make the new relationship pleasant or miserable at times. Remember, your decision will affect how they spend their future holidays, how free they will feel in your new living space, and how memories of their dad are preserved. Think carefully, communicate clearly, and listen attentively. These simple actions will help your children in this new adventure, and make it easier for them and for you.

Money talks. Pinched pennies squeal. Dashing through the dollars sounds more pleasant, but may be destructive. I have observed the marriage of a widow and widower when they worked out money issues with wisdom and consensus, and it was a beautiful thing. But this is not always the case. Having eyes wide open and bank accounts and credit reports on the table are a good way to begin. In other words, know it all, and be willing to live with what's on the table if you choose to remarry. Increasingly, prenuptial agreements are considered to be a wise thing even in Christian marriages, especially in second marriages for "vintage" people. Rather than say you should or should not have such an agreement, I would say get all the information, and make your decision with input from your board of directors.

*Your wish, your decision,
God's call on your life,
are uniquely yours.*

Statistics indicate that most widows remarry. (Remember, our average age is a little over fifty-five.) Widowers are more likely to remarry than widows and do so more quickly. Do these statistics matter? No. Your wish, your decision, God's call on your life, are uniquely yours. If grafting a different branch in a tree takes careful selection and care, imagine how much more important is the decision to embark on a new relationship. Take your time, proceed with caution, and pray much.

I confess to being confused and comforted by this rearranged family tree. I don't know what normal is. Most of my theories have proved to be inadequate to explain the oddities and surprises of life. I've reexamined Scripture and, in a strange way, find great comfort in the realness revealed there: families whose reality did not fit the mold, the expectation of the day.

One morning in my usual habit, I settled into my lawn chair tucked into the little front entryway. With coffee on the side table and the new morning light turning more of the shadows of the valley below me into brilliance, I reread the familiar passage of Jesus' final words before death. Strangely, for the first time, I read of Mary's experience during those hours not just as the mother of Jesus, but as a widow. Why had I never considered her in that role before? Theologians presume Joseph, her husband, to have been older than she was. We know there were other brothers and sisters.

It would have been typical that Jesus, as the eldest son, would take on the care of his mother. In some sense He must have done that. One act of His love for her during His dying hours was to make provision for her future. One would have expected Him to instruct the next oldest brother to care for her. However, His words were, instead, to His best friend, John. "When Jesus saw his mother and the disciple whom he loved standing beside her, he said to his mother, 'Woman, here is your son.' Then he said to the disciple, 'Here is your mother.' And from that hour the disciple took her into his own home" (John 19:26–27 NRSV).

In that harshest of moments, the threshold of death, Jesus cares for His mother. We see that families throughout the ages have had oddities and surprises. I take great comfort in the fact that our shaken, rearranged, puzzling family tree does not surprise our Creator. The storm that shook us just rearranged us and made us stronger.

A BIBLICAL PERSPECTIVE ON GOD'S CARE

Do you wonder if God cares for you? When your family tree quakes, do you wonder if He notices? And what about your children: has He forgotten them? These verses are good reminders of God's heart for us.

- ◆ "He defends the cause of the **fatherless** and the widow, and loves the alien, giving him food and clothing" (Deuteronomy 10:18).
- ◆ "Do not deprive the alien or the **fatherless** of justice, or take the cloak of the widow as a pledge" (Deuteronomy 24:17).
- ◆ "Cursed is the man who withholds justice from the alien, the **fatherless** or the widow. Then all the people shall say, 'Amen!' " (Deuteronomy 27:19).
- ◆ "A father to the **fatherless**, a defender of widows, is God in his holy dwelling" (Psalm 68:5).
- ◆ "The Lord watches over the alien and sustains the **fatherless** and the widow, but he frustrates the ways of the wicked" (Psalm 146:9).

Knowing our Father's heart does not guarantee that His will *will* be done on earth. Oh, how I wish that were true. Especially when I see the plight of widows in other countries, I am quite aware that this is the world, not heaven. And we're not getting it right here. Just as death was not a part of His plan for us, injustice and hurt are not His desire either. Remember, this is not God's final chapter. He can show our children love in ways we could never imagine. He can send us tender mercies from surprising places. He can grow and heal our tree—not in spite of our, loss but through it.

I took this picture while hiking above Flagstaff, Arizona. How unlikely to discover an evergreen growing through a stone. It spoke to me of God's promise to be able to bring good from all things. Harsh circumstances need not prevent growth. In fact, the aqua tint to this evergreen had a beauty unique from all the trees around it. Our family tree, growing through hard places, can be beautiful.

Section Four

The NEW YOU—
THE NEW WOMAN
IN THE MIRROR:
DIFFERENT AND STRONG

Chapter Eight

FINDING YOURSELF:
"I Didn't Know You."

———— ⊶∞⊷ ————

"Lord, make me see Thy glory in every place."
—MICHELANGELO
"... including myself" (ADDED BY MIRIAM NEFF)

Who is in that strange image looking back at me from the window? The woman engulfed in a canyon of Chicago's glass and concrete buildings looks pale. The night seems especially dark as she approaches the bridge over the Chicago River on her way to the train station. The hood on her long black coat is not enough to keep the wind from chilling her neck and telling her shoulders that three layers are not enough. Her stride is long and determined. She grips the shoulder strap of her purse as if it might be a weapon of protection if need be. This is not the woman who was accustomed to being squired about town to concerts and other pleasures by her husband. Whether she should be walking alone is a moot point. This is her new life. But who is she, this new person? Will she emerge . . . or must I discover or create her? Those questions will have to wait.

I need to lengthen my stride to catch the next train.

Two truths and two lies. Have you ever played this game? You make four statements about yourself, two true things and two lies. The audience guesses what is real about you and what you made up. In this get-acquainted game, even close friends learn new things about each other. Did she really start driving at the age of twelve on a Minneapolis-Moline tractor? Was she really in the Miss Indiana University pageant? This makes for a fun game with lots of laughs when the truth is revealed.

If I were playing this game today, I could confuse myself! What is now true about me and what is not? What remains and what is changed? You probably understand. At this stage we may feel like life is somehow a game, and what is real cannot have really happened. We can list four things that are true, wishing that the option "I am single" was not true, but it is. Before we might have stated, "I love solitude." Now we dread it. We might have said before, "I am seldom fearful." Now we have a strange sense of disquiet entering our own home alone at night—for no reason.

In fact, if the descriptions must be current, we hardly know what to say. Many of us, myself included, discover upon becoming a widow that we don't know who we are! What is still true of this new woman? What has changed? Had you said before that I would still be water-skiing doubles with my grandsons, I would not be surprised. What *is* surprising, however, is that Edmond and I smile at each other over the wake and we're both wearing braces! Yes, we have the same orthodontist! This new life is rather like entering adolescence again.

The search for self is nothing new. Three thousand years ago Solomon pointed out that there is nothing new under the sun (Ecclesiastes 1:9). Thousands of books have been written on the search, varying from the Bible to *Dibs in Search of Self*,[13] to Richard Bolles's *What Color Is Your Parachute?*[14]. What takes us by surprise is that we once had the answer to that question. And now we do not. I was certainly taken by surprise by my confusion about who I was after Bob's death. I had no idea that with his departure, the person I once was would be obsolete, not only to those around me, but for the challenges and opportunities I now faced.

UNIQUE, NOT UNIFORM

A seemingly easy answer, and one we might first grasp, is to be like others around us. For some reason, we humans fear being different. It is that "other than Christlikeness" that creeps in and clutches us by the neck saying, "Fit in!" Just as we entered adolescence fearing uniqueness (the pressure to conform gripped us tightly then), we enter this phase often with the same fears. We must hold tightly to the truth that our uniqueness, whatever we discover it to be, is a blessing given us by our Creator for our good, delight, and enjoyment. One never-changing truth repeatedly emphasized in Scripture is this: We are unique. Read about it in passages such as Psalm 139:13–16, Ephesians 2:10, and 1 Corinthians 12.

We can look at others around us, question, pray, and listen. Our goal is not to imitate them, but to gain wisdom to apply in our new life. Let's look back at what we've already said about this task of finding ourselves. Earlier we laid a foundation for discovery. In chapter 2 about fear, we examined our board of directors. You may have invited some to exit and invited others to a seat at your table. They give us helpful feedback. Often they see strengths that are invisible to us because of the fog of numbness that surrounds us at times. They may see weaknesses that we are inclined to embrace when we dread moving forward. They are another set of eyes to our world. Good board members prod us to move forward—be real, be engaged. We need them.

In chapter 4 we discovered that our new life is an *opportunity* to change. We created our personal inventory of things we did in the past. While this exercise helps us identify what we can do, we also feel the stirrings of a new sense within us. What did we enjoy? What sparked a passion in our soul? What was worth the annoying early alarm noise? When we woke up in the middle of the night for seemingly no reason, what was worth thinking about? What was worth getting up, researching possibilities, and journaling about—even in a cold house? What motivates us to bundle into our fuzzy robe, push our shivering toes into those worn house slippers that conform wonderfully to every misshaped lump on our feet (and should never, never be thrown out)? What stimulates us to start the coffeepot instead of burrowing back under the covers?

We needn't feel apologetic about exploring what we've done. The Bible often references people by their tasks, what they contributed through their work. Lydia in the book of Acts was a seller of purple. Mary and Martha hospitably opened their home to others. Priscilla and Aquila were tentmakers. Benaiah was a warrior, and Abigail a competent manager of an extensive household.

There are lots of tools today that can help us in this exploration. Tests that help us research careers that would be compatible to our abilities and interests also give us glimpses of many other aspects of ourselves. Some are available online, and a host of others can be accessed through counseling centers. One online example is Dr. John Holland's Self-Directed Search at www.self-directed-search.com. Another resource is the classic book *What Color Is Your Parachute?* by Richard Bolles, which offers a myriad of ideas for self-exploration. His Web site www.jobhuntersbible.com also offers assessment tools. Most of these assessments cost less than a new item for your wardrobe and have longer-lasting value for the new you. While all these tools may help you know yourself, they should not be used to *define* the new you. Helpful? Yes. Prescriptive? No. Informative? Absolutely.

> *One of the great*
> *challenges for widows*
> *is to think outside the box.*

One of the great challenges for widows is to think outside the box. Our experience in the valley of the shadow of death tempts us to shrink in fear and find a very small zone of comfort in which we can hide, hoping to heal there. Wrong. Hiding does not bring healing. In that cocoon, fear grows, depression can become permanent, and the huge possibilities of our future will never be realized. What we did and who we were in the past may be our foundation, but they do not define our future.

I was recently surprised to be affirmed in my own journey from an unexpected source. I had been invited to Selma, Alabama, by Rob Moore, station manager of Moody South radio stations. They were dedicating a new tower, WRNF, named in honor of my husband. With great anticipation, I flew to Montgomery, picked up my rental car, and discovered I had a few hours to spare before meeting at a church for the caravan up to the new tower. I drove to Selma, walked the Edmund Pettus Park at the famous bridge of Bloody Sunday, and visited the National Voting Rights Museum. I entered in a different way a world I never knew. Time stood still and raced at the same time. I was back in the sixties seeing the newspaper headlines, standing in the reproduction of a jail cell, seeing the garb of the Klansmen. I ached with shame at our behavior, one human being to another—all descendants of Adam and Eve— and many of us members of the same body of Christ, the church, the body where we are instructed to care for each and all members.

A glance at my watch disrupted my exploration. Time dictated that I had to scramble for a lukewarm, drugstore cup of coffee and an aging sweet roll mashed in my purse from breakfast. I devoured this lunch on the way to the assigned meeting point for the dedication of precious WRNF. Upon arriving at the church for the caravan, I asked Pastor James Jackson, reverend of Brown's Chapel, if I could ride with him and get better acquainted on the trip. His friend Reverend Lionel Melton, of Perryville Baptist Church, joined us. We spoke of the political happenings in our country, the elections, the status of unity within the body of Christ today, as well as about our individual journeys. They knew of my recent loss of Bob and were quite interested in all I am doing today. I acknowledged my own surprise at my life today, my Web ministry, writing, my sense of freedom and new boldness.

Reverend Lionel leaned forward and spoke quietly with his Southern softness. "Mrs. Miriam, it was in you all the time. Now it's time to come out." Reverend Jackson nodded in agreement. My soul was affirmed by this brother-believer God had dropped into my life for one day, to assure me it was all in God's plan from the moment I was conceived.

TRANSFORMED, NOT CONFORMED

It's been in you all the time. Crisis has happened. What will come of this? I don't mean, what will become of your living space, your finances, your schedule, and all that external stuff of life. All those will change and we address that in these pages, and they matter. But more important is what will happen *within* you? What is happening *in* me? We have a choice to be conformed to the ordinary, the expected, the easier path. Or we can choose to let this event transform us. It is as if we have come to a fork in the road.

One wide path ahead looks like this:

◆ Do the expected. Quickly look for other people to fill the void of our loneliness.

◆ Look around for someone else to take the financial reins of our situation.

◆ Let anger languish in our soul since it takes too much energy to evict it.

◆ Trust the grey of depression to shield us from the bright yellow and red of hurt and woundedness.

We can't turn back. Our past path is forever closed. We hear the gentle reminder of Paul saying, "Do not conform any longer to the pattern of this world, but be transformed by the renewing of your mind" (Romans 12:2).

We have a better option. Most people are merely conformed—but we can be transformed. Think of how many charities got started—many are the result of crisis transformed into a mission. Breast cancer survivors groups, parents raising awareness and supporting research for autism, organizations for finding missing children—the list is practically endless. And those movements were not started by a happy, trouble-free individual waking up one sunshiny morning saying, "I think I'll do something nice today. My schedule is clear, I have time, energy, and money to spare. I think I'll start a hard project bringing attention to a little-known problem.

I'll invest hours, energy, my own postage stamps, and gasoline. And the results will be huge, instantaneous, rewarding, and apparent to all." Rarely do great missions rise from easy circumstances.

Transformed people put their shoulder to the plow, which is impossible to do if you are facing backwards. While new missions may be about someone's action, their *doing*, something happened before that; something *inside* them. Something happened in their *being*. While we'll talk about finding our mission in the next chapter, that mission cannot be started without an inner conviction that yesterday's crisis must not be wasted.

Yes, we may be getting soaked under the waterfall of disaster. But others see the mist produced by water pounding us and they see through the resulting prism to see a rainbow. They see hope. They see promise that leads to a reward beyond what their eyes can see. We often hear that the end of the rainbow, which, of course, we can never see due to the arc of the earth, touches a pot of gold. We know that's not true. But the charm of the idea evokes songwriters to pen music and poets to become eloquent. We who are believers do not need the fantasy of the pot of gold. We grasp the reality of the rainbow, which is God's promise to us. Storms turn eventually to sunlight. This declining earth is temporary. Heaven is ahead.

We don't just hope He'll do a good thing in us as the result of what we've been through. We *know* He will because He has promised He will. Isaiah 61:3 tells us He will "provide for those who grieve in Zion—to bestow on them a crown of **beauty** instead of **ashes**, the oil of gladness instead of mourning, and a garment of praise instead of a spirit of despair. They will be called oaks of righteousness, a planting of the Lord for the display of his splendor."

Our Creator is a transformation specialist. We're in good hands. I know because Scripture says I can be a new and different person (our Romans 12: 2 principle). Sure now in the knowledge that He'll be the power to change me, it's safe to ask the question:

Q Who would I like to be?

A I'd like to be like Christ.

Q What is He like?

A He loves everybody. He does not discriminate. He made the world a better place by what He said and did. He taught as much by His actions as by His words.

Q How does that translate into my behavior?

A For starters, here's how I'd like to see my life transformed:

I'd like to have a love for poor and rich alike, every race, for people who seem to have done it all right, and for those who have messed up. I'd like to leave this world a better place because I drove that tractor (yes, that was true), because I counseled in the public high schools, because I sang "Climb Every Mountain" as my "talent" in the Miss IU pageant. (Now that was a true disaster—I represented my sorority, albeit poorly, and appropriately lost.)

Can I? Yes, I can. Two verses in Proverbs describe my options.

"If you falter in times of trouble, how small is your strength!" (Proverbs 24:10).

The word *falter* means crumble from within or succumb to the circumstance. That is one of my options as a woman who really would rather not be a widow.

"For though a righteous woman falls seven times, she rises again" (Proverbs 24:16a).

The word *fall* means to be tripped up. This is an external thing. Yes, our circumstance may mean we temporarily fall. But we do not stay down. If our finances seem tangled, we will sort them out. If we are immobilized by grief, it will be temporary. If we are lonely, we will discover new, appropriate sources of comfort. The number seven in Scripture refers to completeness. The implication is that there is no external circumstance that will keep us down. No matter how many circumstances trip us, falling is not permanent. We can falter from the inside out, but nothing in the outside circumstances of our world will keep us down. We have a guarantee of transformation if we want it. Now let's look at the new you.

THE NEW YOU

You and I have two unique new factors in our lives: the death of our husbands and a different relationship to God because of our widowhood. Both of these new factors have a profound impact on who we are today. These are not the only new things. But we all have at least these. Let's look at how these factors change us.

Our loss

Humans simply do not experience crisis without being changed by it. When we meet a person and discover she has experienced the loss that we have, we sense a common bond. In our widows group, we feel free to share the impact our husband's death had on us. Our healing moves forward as we tell our story. There are those "aha" moments as we realize we are not alone. Another human being felt that feeling. We call it our sorority that no one wants to join. When a new woman joins our circle, at the same time that we welcome her warmly, we tell her we're sorry she's here. And we all laugh together because we all understand the humor in our contradiction! While the grief and loss that we experience is unique, much of the feeling is similar to any other person's hurt from suffering loss.

Humans simply do not experience crisis without being changed by it.

Widows do not have a corner on the "hurt" market. Divorce is a death of sorts, and the 75 percent departure of our friendship network is true of divorcées as well. Job loss, a shattered career, financial disaster, an unwelcome geographic move, all tear at the fabric of your being and require that you change to accommodate the new realities in your life.

In our losses, regardless of their cause, we share some of the same new realities. Here are some typical changes. They may not all be true of you, but you can probably relate to some.

- ◆ We no longer trust in people and things we trusted before.
- ◆ We have a different, more real view of death.
- ◆ We have a different and more real curiosity about heaven. We contemplate more intensely what life after this life will be like.
- ◆ We have a real investment in heaven that brings us to think of it more.
- ◆ We treasure small joys overlooked by others.
- ◆ We embrace today, realizing tomorrow is not a sure thing.
- ◆ We see people who have suffered with a new empathy and compassion.

Dee Brestin, whom I quoted in chapter 5, articulated the result of these new realities in her life after the death of her husband. After talking about her desire to be around people who know and understand suffering, she talks about people who stay with us through our transition from bitter to sweet.

Dee says, "They see my invisible knife. They stay by my side when I am not pleasant and listen to me drone on. They've been there so they know better than to tell me God is sovereign and all things will work together for the good. I know that's true, but I don't want to hear it now. High-tide grief is not the time to speak solutions. (Women who have had miscarriages tell me the last thing they want to hear is: 'You can have another baby.') When one is grieving, it is the time to be silent, to hug, and to weep. I don't know why it divides the grief to have someone weep with you, but it does. Friends like this are like Ruth, who, having lost her own dear husband, could stand beside Naomi without trying to fix the unfixable. Ruth listened again and again to Naomi's heartache, steadfastly

staying at her side, knowing that if she did not grow weary in loving her mother-in-law, in God's time, the woman who was saying,
'Call me Bitter!' would become sweet again."

How accurately Dee describes us! We are now more likely to
cry with others in their pain. We offer a tissue and a hug instead of
"fix-it" advice and Scripture verses hurled like darts because we feel
we need to *say* something. We are more sensitive, appropriate, and
compassionate, not in spite of our loss but because of it. We are
compassionate because our heart has been broken. Ordinary comforts that were adequate in our life before are inadequate for today.
That is precisely why God steps in and gives us His comfort. As we
said earlier, He does it in ways both understandable and surprising. He does it in ways He comforts others and ways unique to only
us (2 Corinthians 1:3–4).

May I share one of my ordinary stories of God's comfort? In
the last months of Bob's life, the late Chicago winter days were bitter cold and he could not "walk" with me around the circle, as we
called the two-mile neighborhood walk we had shared for years.
We always enjoyed spotting deer and kept a count of how many we
saw. I'm not sure why. We just did. Though his powerful wheelchair
meant we frequently made the walk during his battle with ALS,
eventually cold temperatures meant it was unsafe to go. I would occasionally scurry out alone, leaving Bob with our children or his
excellent caregiver Edgar. The cold would clear my head, and I
could cry without being seen. I always reported back to Bob the
deer count of the day.

After his exit to heaven, on one particularly bad day when my
future seemed bleak, grieving seemed endless, and the winter un-
relentingly cold and long, I threw on my coat, a head shawl, and
Bob's gloves and went out to walk wherever the neighborhood
lanes led. Hmmm, two deer at the pond. I walked on. Five more
deer in the woods on the hill. Two more in a neighbor's yard din-
ing on bushes. Each time, I paused to stare and remember that Bob
would not be there for my report on the deer. The ache in my heart
moved upward to become a softball-like knot in my throat. Hot
tears could wash away neither. When I spotted number twenty-two,

I realized that Bob and I had never seen that many deer on a walk before! I stopped counting. With God's gentle nudging, He had my attention.

Aren't you amazed, Miriam, that I see you, I know you, and I know you were comforted by counting deer? Did you think that I, too, would forget you now that you are alone? Did you think that your cloak of grief that separates you from others hides you from My watchful eye? Oh, no, My dear child. I see you. I will walk beside you as your eyes search for deer. I know what will warm your soul. I already know every step you will take. I will be your confidant. You have ME!

The long winter days were still bitter cold. But God's comfort became more real because of the deer count that day. I bought a new flavored coffee that helped bring on spring. (Or maybe the caffeine just gave my skin a warm rush!) The result was that I had more comfort, so much that I just had to start passing it on.

Our new relationship with our Creator

"Thank you for joining us this morning. We'd like to know who you are and how we can minister to you. Complete the register and . . ." The voice from the church platform fades into the background and the white noise of my dilemma rumbles in my mind. I stare at the form:

"Name: Miriam Neff"
(That was easy.)
"___ Married ___ Single ___ Widowed"
(Yes, this is the hard part.)

More than two years after the death of my husband of forty-one years, my hand still refuses to check the box for *widow*. Yes, I live alone now and recently received my first e-mail invitation to a singles ministry function. I pushed *delete* immediately because I am very much Mrs. Bob Neff, and very much married, thank you. I'm all three! I mark no box and read on.

"How can we pray for you this week?" The question is followed by five lines. Let's see, how can I condense the drama in my new life? One son is considering accepting a job in another country. Another was just let go from his treasured calling of following in his father's footsteps. Two more adult children face significant life decisions. (All without their dad, who was their sounding board, their voice of reason, the one who listened with intense, gentle eye contact as they spilled their stuff onto his grid of wisdom.) Also, I think a raccoon has acquired my chimney as his new home. Why not? The space is available to my masked friend. Who needs a cozy fire when there's no one to snuggle with? And—eeks—it's starting to snow and I haven't raked the leaves yet.

Okay, this is not going to fit in five lines. The next person in the pew is looking at me, probably wondering why I can't fill in a few simple blanks. I write nothing, smile sheepishly, and pass the register on. I said it earlier, and it's still the truth: I do not like the label *widow*.

> *God holds me more
> closely to His heart
> because of this new status.*

However, I am discovering something good about being a widow; in fact, it is grand. God holds me more closely to His heart because of this new status. Yes, this is true and unbelievable. While in most circles here we have become invisible, or nearly so, we have become precious to God. He states that fact in no uncertain terms from the Old Testament through the New Testament.

There are 103 Scripture references to widows, revealing that we are not invisible to God. As we study those verses, with gratitude and amazement we discover that we are not only close to God's heart, but He measures everyone by how they treat us (James 1:27.) This is both a comforting and sobering insight. Widows, orphans, prisoners—the voiceless—God chooses to speak for us.

He instructs that our needs be met (Deuteronomy 24:17) through the church's tithes if necessary (Deuteronomy 14:28–29; 26:12; Acts 6:1–4). He instructs that in our vulnerability we be given our legal rights (Isaiah 1:17; Luke 18:1–8). He commends us for our sacrificial giving (Mark 12:42–43). He tells our story—the widow at Zarephath and her generosity (1 Kings 17:9), the prophet's widow, her pot of oil, her faith and obedience (2 Kings 4:1–7).

In the Old Testament, the story of widows Naomi and Ruth showcases loyalty in a description so poetic, the standard has been repeated doubtless in thousands, if not millions, of weddings. When Naomi urged her widowed daughter-in-law to return to her own people, Ruth replied, "Don't urge me to leave you or to turn back from you. Where you go I will go, and where you stay I will stay. Your people will be my people and your God my God. Where you die I will die, and there I will be buried. May the Lord deal with me, be it ever so severely, if anything but death separates you and me" (Ruth 1:16–17). Ruth's loss was real, her loyalty intense, and her willingness to step into a new life, an example to us all.

Jesus showed His disciples what real giving was, not by pointing out the wealthy Pharisees and Sadducees who tithed even minute amounts of their spice crops, but the poor widow who gave her two mites—and was not embarrassed to do so, given the method in which they presented their gifts in that day.

As I studied Scripture on widows these themes emerged:

To the widow

◆ Be generous regardless of the quantity of your possessions, since no one's stuff is her own anyway.
◆ Be filled with faith—you can't help but be when you see how special you are to your Creator who is your new husband.

To the church

◆ The significance of your church is not in its numbers but that its priorities match those of God.
◆ The character of your leaders is not measured by their popularity or power but by their attention and care for the powerless and voiceless among them—widows, orphans, and prisoners.

To summarize my discoveries in Scripture about widows, our new reality has ushered us into an up close and personal relationship with our Creator. Oh, yes, we have changed. Though each of our stories are different, we all share the common understanding of a loss that is final beyond description. There will be no phone call, no plane delayed but still landing, no second chance to right our past regrets. Sitting curled up on the cold ground clutching my knees to my chest, watching the gardener gently work the grass seed into the fresh dirt on my husband's grave set me apart forever from the life I once had. Other widows understand that.

We have, at the same time, been invited into an intimate relationship with our Creator beyond description. His listening ear, His defending touch, His comforting arms transform us into faith-filled, generous, and compassionate women. I trust that you allow what God has written about us and how He treasures us to give you a new sense of worth and a solid conviction that this new you is treasured, equipped, and ready to take the next step of finding your mission in this new life.

Chapter Nine

*F*INDING YOUR MISSION:
A Purpose Worth Living For
"I didn't know I could."

---∞∞∞---

"Aim for heaven and you will get earth thrown in.
Aim for earth and you get neither."
—C. S. LEWIS

*T*he unthinkable has happened. All has changed. In our case, we are alone now. We are not unique in experiencing crisis. As we said earlier, many others have faced cataclysmic change. Divorce, financial upheaval or disaster, the death of a child, disability, the death of dreams—life comes hard. While we as widows don't have a corner on the crisis market, our journey to moving forward is unique in some ways. During the first months we simply survive. We sort, we cry, we do what must be done that day. But eventually, most of us find a common question tapping at the edges of our minds. "Will I have purpose in my new life as a widow?"

Our shaken faith requires that we find the answer. Most widows, even the most spiritually grounded ones, admit to at least a quiver in their faith. We'll talk about that in the next chapter. But first, let's address the important question of purpose and meaning in our life today. We have two options:

To stay in the tattered space of our life clutching at the torn remnants of our past, mourning the empty spaces, breathing the stagnate air of yesterday, OR

To create a new pattern of living, a new reason to face a new day, to choose meaning and relevance for tomorrow; in summary, to find our unique and new mission in life.

CONSIDERING THE OPTIONS

We can discover and shape a new life with new purpose. I prefer to see it as our mission. It's our reason to face tomorrow; our contribution to the people and place we are in; it's our way to give back for the blessings we have experienced. In other words, it's our assignment, our ambition, our calling.

What can I promise you when you create your new mission?

- ◆ I cannot promise you quiet, but I can promise peace.
- ◆ I cannot promise material comfort, but I can promise meaning.
- ◆ I cannot promise health, but I can promise soul satisfaction.

First, let me reassure you that your confusion about your purpose in this new life is not unusual. Given our culture where often wives shape their lives around their husband's life, becoming a widow leaves a larger void than if we were in a more egalitarian culture. I'm not making a judgment on this, but rather simply acknowledging that it is true. I understand. Remember, this farm girl moved to Chicago because of her husband's calling to serve God through Christian broadcasting in a Chicago-based organization. Forty-three years later, Bob is in heaven and I'm still here!

E-mails to my ministry are often peppered with questions about meaning and heartache over not just the void of being alone, but the absence of so many activities and relationships that gave meaning to our days when we were a couple. The problem seems even more acute the more involved husbands were in ministry. My heart goes out to pastors' wives, many of whom seem especially adrift upon becoming a widow. Often their world revolved around their husband's work, and their work was volunteer (no personal health insurance, Social Security, or other benefits). One such widow found herself with less than five dollars in the bank account, and had no insurance or other assets. And they are especially vulnerable to the dilemmas I cite next.

OUR MISSIONS ARE DIFFERENT

Our new mission may be tied to our circumstances upon becoming a widow. My friend Susan, whose five children were ages three through sixteen when David died, is and will be totally engrossed in parenting her children alone. Spiritual instruction, school, athletics, and the regular care of family will be her mission for years.

Barbara, whose husband was a talented sculptor, has started new businesses, one related to his work, and others that he had envisioned to sustain their family. With two teenage daughters and her entrepreneurial spirit, her days are full.

Lynn Cole had founded with her husband, Andrew, a ministry called Rise International. They began building schools in Angola, Africa, the country where Andrew grew up with missionary parents Don and Naomi Cole. Andrew exited suddenly to heaven at age fifty. Lynn continues the ministry. Their four children are involved, as well as a host of other supporters and partners who shared the vision she and Andrew had. While Lynn would have never imagined herself as the sole leader of a thriving, continually growing outreach in Africa, she is! To date they have built 114 schools, 25 partnering with Andrew, and 89 since his departure to heaven. Obviously, this is one woman on a mission!

Jane's pastor husband was killed in Iraq. The incredible hardships she endured to get him home for burial were beyond what I can fathom. Then she courageously undertook to thank over seven hundred people personally, writing her own cards and letters, letting them know of her appreciation for their support. But eventually she faced the new unknown. She had been a teacher in the church school and an active partner in ministry. Their church graciously enabled her to stay in the parsonage for a year to heal and seek God's next step for her. This courageous woman moved to Florida, beginning a job in a Christian law firm. Her daughter attends college nearby. The demands of her job are extensive enough that she often welcomes staying at work on Friday evenings to wrap things up. She, like many of us, struggle with those Friday night hours. In fact, the whole weekend in those early years is unlikely to be a good time for us.

In appendix A you'll read about Marie, who is the mother of eight. She reluctantly took on the role of single parent and found it especially hard to be the head of the household with her children ages seven months to seventeen years old. Her family transitioned from homeschooling to public schools, and she is working part-time as a caregiver and is also cleaning houses for friends. Her life dictates her mission. She parents, and is the breadwinner, the provider. I was blessed to receive her Christmas letter complete with family picture. What an awesome woman!

Lynne C., a mother of five children, moved, started nursing school, has gone on some medical mission trips, and is vibrantly involved in her children. This is an amazing accomplishment given that one is in the military going to Iraq, one in medical school, and others testing their young adult legs in living independently.

Ewa Brycko and her husband had started a Christian radio station in Ostrada, Poland, when Mirek died suddenly of a heart attack. Bob and I were scheduled to visit this ministry four short months after his death. We arrived in Warsaw to be hosted in her home before we traveled to the station. The several-hour drive was an adventure like no other. I can only summarize by saying there were four lanes of traffic on three tight lanes of road with people crowded on the edges selling tableclothes and food, and with others riding bicycles and walking. How Ewa kept her speed and sanity, I do not know. After visiting the station, recording a program, meeting the mayor of Ostrada and a church family of supporters, it was time to make the drive back. The night now was black, and pounding drops of rain announced an impending downpour. Ewa approached the *nondrivers* side of the car and stated simply to my husband, "You drive."

Did she know he'd never driven on roads like this with rules (???) like theirs? He crumpled his tall body behind the steering wheel into the small car. She settled in the front seat. I, trying to cover my fear, leaned up and said to her, "Do you trust my husband to drive us home?" "No," she quietly stated. "I trust God." And with that she promptly fell asleep for the duration of the drive.

I, on the other hand, with white knuckles, gripped a rolled-up magazine, prayed, and looked in terror at the vehicles careering around us from front and behind. Thankfully the dark and rain moved the people away from the roadside shoulders so Bob could swerve there when necessary. Ten years later, the radio station is thriving, Ewa is remarried, and I stand in awe of her faith in those early months as a widow! I also stand in awe at the fact that she hosted us and educated us on their ministry just four months after her tragic loss. I now understand that her body demanded sleep for the road trip back to Warsaw on that rainy night in Poland.

PAST HISTORY—PART OF THE NEW MYSTERY

I trust as you read these stories you see the connections from their lives before to their new life today. You may also be saying, "Wow, they did big things! I'm not like that. There's no leader within. My children are grown. Our lives were more ordinary, and so am I." Remember, we are all different. And our past does not dictate our future. It is likely, too, that these women, before they were widows and probably in the first few months of their lives alone, would not have fathomed the things they would be doing and the inner strength that rose when necessity demanded that they stand alone.

You may also be saying,
"Wow, they did big things!
I'm not like that."

Remember the slingshot principle we learned from David? The principle is relevant here. He killed Goliath with his slingshot after declining Saul's armor and sword. They did not fit. He explained, "I cannot go in these." He was available and successful with what he knew, his small hunting weapon rather than a large sword. Later, when running from Saul, he was offered as a weapon Goliath's sword, which would have been much larger than Saul's. "There's none like it. Give it to me." Life had changed David's skills. Wars, marriage, a loyal friendship—the adult David was not the same man as the boy who faced Goliath. The skills of the young man were adequate for that contest. And he grew from there to become a great warrior and king.

The slingshot principle, simply stated, is this: When you use the skill you have, God gives you an upgrade. Times of crisis are your opportunity to use the skills you have. Tomorrow will be a new day.

One of God's favorite challenges to us is to consider what we are holding in our hands. "Then the Lord said to him, 'What is that in your hand?' 'A staff,' he replied" (Exodus 4:2). God started Moses on an incredible journey of leadership showing him that He would use what Moses possessed. God would use Moses' tools in ways he had never experienced before. Moses would do things he'd never done before. In fact, his life would be miracle-sprinkled—some events for all to see, and some private and shared only between Moses and God.

Can you believe that would be possible in your own life? Perhaps you don't see it today. But keep reading with your mind open to the possibility that new things ahead will be good.

Another of God's challenges to us is to approach what we do with vigor. First Samuel 10:7 tells us, "Do whatever your hand finds to do, for God is with you." Ecclesiastes 9:10 similarly says, "Whatever your hand finds to do, do it with all your might." This almost seems like an oxymoron for a widow. Our energy is small, our vision may not be clear, and hesitance seems to be our new middle name.

I understand. In my first summer alone I needed to have repairs made to both front and back entrances to my home. Following the advice of my board of directors, I got three estimates. I actually decided which one would be the wisest choice for the job. And then I did nothing! I just could not initiate the project. Now another winter is passed and the need is greater than ever. Aging outdoor carpeting has crumpled and torn, and cement is crumbling, challenging my guests to step over the mess. Yes, I've made some phone calls, and I will act this time. Scripture reassures me that God does care about even the mundane things in our lives. I simply need to put this widow's might into it and move forward.

When you learned about the new you, you looked at the assessments from chapter 4 and recognized that you have some positive personal habits from your past. You also identified skills you discovered and developed before. Whether these were in jobs, volunteer work, or in your role of wife or mother, they are still things you are able to do. These are tools you possess. They can be refined and/or used as stepping-stones in a new mission.

You created a list of things you'd like to do. Now that you've read and pondered chapter 8, where we looked at the new you, let's visit that list again. Can you see now that some of those dreams are worth reaching for? My widower friend Jo, a Marine, uses a phrase that describes him and the training he has received to be part of the most effective fighting unit in the world. "We are hardwired and soft wired to improvise, adapt, and overcome." If the United States Marine Corps can do that using human drills and development, can't widows achieve the same given the special position we have with our Creator?

Remember, too, that we have some new truths to lean into that we studied in chapter 4. Just for reminders:

- ◆ We are more resilient than we think. It's His day, His calendar, and His group.
- ◆ New friends will be discovered in new ways and in new places.
- ◆ God is creative in His plan for us.

While these truths might have seemed remote when you first started reading this book, I hope that you are now embracing the fact that this new role in life (while not of our choosing, fraught with surprises and challenges) *is* our opportunity to change. We have free time and flexibility we did not have before. This is precisely the ideal place for new missions to be born. If your list of things you'd like to do is short, and you look at my list of ideas in chapter 4 and none of them spark an interest in your soul, here's another idea.

We have free time and flexibility we did not have before.

Look at your local newspaper and determine things around you that could be better. Today, our news highlighted the statistic that the dropout rate in high school is high. Detroit public schools, for example, were listed as having a 75 percent dropout rate. You needn't read lengthy articles to know beyond imagining that the future for these precious adolescents is dim.

What might you do? Usually, with a little research, you will find a program nearby that assists students. Some are based in local libraries, YMCAs, or churches. Can you listen to students read? check their homework? (They are not likely to be doing calculus. If you can add, subtract, and work with a calculator, you'll be helpful.) Can you show up regularly and encourage them to be faithful school- and tutor-session attenders? You may be the connection that helps one of these precious adolescents stay in school.

Our widow's mite becomes a widow's might!

Our news today mentioned that the economics of today are creating even more hardships for those who were already struggling. Food pantries and thrift shops often are an important lifeline. One church magazine noted that many of their food pantries were bare. And usually these ministries need volunteers. Can you sort and label? You may discover more needs that can be addressed.

The principle of using what is in your hand usually leads to the development of new skills and interests. We begin somewhere.

The thrill of productivity and seeing that we have something to offer, whether in a new job or volunteer role, prompts us to apply ourselves and do what is before us with all our might. Our widow's mite becomes a widow's might! You might use your coupon and bargain hunting skills as a food shopper to expand your grocery budget productivity to supply yourself *and* take food to a pantry for others.

Needs are endless in our own communities. When we look outward, we discover more. My trip to Ouagadougou, Burkina Faso, opened my eyes to the plight of widows and children in Africa. I came home with the recognition that, though the plight of many widows in the United States is unfortunate, we are wealthy, healthy, and have options far beyond those of most widows in the world.

I listened, through interpreter Joanna, to the stories of women who toil endlessly and still have not earned enough to feed their children. Yet their faith is joy-filled and they have courage beyond my imagination. They love their children and struggle creatively to stay afloat in the harshest of conditions. In fact, they have inspired me to dream that someday I can participate in connecting widows here with widows in other countries so that we can mutually sustain and encourage each other.

Yet another opportunity for mission surfaced as I read a recent newsletter, *The Christian Legal Alert*, published by the Gibbs family. Their review of our communities in our country noted that in the past Christians were actively involved in their communities, on committees, local government positions, and boards. This need is even greater today. Imagine your impact by participating in your local library, serving as a volunteer and perhaps on a board. Why not attend a village or city meeting and get acquainted with the leaders and important issues of your community? Does this seem daunting? Just show up and listen. God usually initiates His work with small beginnings fueled by personal passion.

Ideas? They can spring from your daily paper, looking around your community, and daydreaming with God. If you are willing, they will come.

FROM MYSTERY TO MISSION: WRITING
YOUR PERSONAL MISSION STATEMENT

Several years ago I was challenged to write my personal mission statement. This is a variation of what Richard Bolles proposes in *What Color Is Your Parachute?*. While it is a good exercise for anyone, I think it is especially helpful for us in our new life. Rarely could we do this exercise in our early months of being alone. However, on our own timetable, I think this is a helpful tool.

Let's start with an overview of how to write your personal mission statement.

Definition: A personal mission statement is brief, descriptive, and reflects how you were created.

Consider the following:

1. What tasks have I done that brought great satisfaction?
2. What tasks do I look forward to doing?
3. What personal values are important enough to me to motivate me to act when there is no apparent reward or positive feedback for my action?
4. What activities in my life give me that feeling of anticipation, energy, and "I can't wait to get to it"?

Complete these statements:

1. I am energized when I'm looking forward to:
2. I would like to be remembered as a person who:
3. Past accomplishments that I treasure include:

For example, on October 18, 1999, I wrote this statement for myself: *To encourage women in biblical living and be salt in my public high school.* At that time I was a high school counselor and taught a Bible study in my church. Life has changed; I am now retired after my twenty-six-year career in public high schools. I have a new mission statement today.

You may have never created a personal mission statement in the past. Often our lives just happen. Schooling, work, family, caring for others, more work. You may have never felt the need to create a mission statement. One is certainly not necessary to have a productive and fulfilling life. But if you feel yourself floundering, facing the future without much focus or enthusiasm, this can be a beneficial exercise.

I hope you take the time to settle into your favorite easy chair with a notebook and this assignment, and make these lists. Then let the lists settle for a day or two. What else comes to mind? What answers seem not so important as they did at that moment? Next, talk to a few friends who know you well, or maybe some on your board of directors. Do they see a match in your lists and the person they know? The final mission statement is yours alone to create, but others can provide insights and ideas.

A COMMON MISSION

Our Saturday morning Bible study has concluded. We fill our coffee cups again and replenish our fruit and coffee cake plates. (Yes, Luke, the chef at our church, spoils us royally with his treats for our widows Bible study!) In our small groups we ask the usual question, "What's new this month?" At our table today, four of the six women have significant employment issues they are facing. One works part-time for a small shop that is closing. That income, though small, makes her life today possible. It also provides a rhythm to her calendar, a reason to be out and about, given that her daughter lives several states away. Another, a relatively new widow, has not been working and now realizes that her financial situation requires that she earn income. She worries that she does not have marketable skills and is reluctant even to start the interview process. Another works in a medical-related field that is rapidly changing, as will her job. Another will soon retire and needs to supplement that income to maintain a balanced budget. Each is living in the tension of "What will happen next, and how will this turn out?" And, "God has proved Himself dependable so far. I think He still will!" These are words more easily said than lived.

For each of these women, part of their mission statement includes creating and maintaining a balanced personal budget. This may or may not mean that they will be working at their dream job.

They may, as I did, work in a setting of compromise, stress, with some things I loved (working with teens), and other things that were challenging (administrative agendas promoting gay and lesbian lifestyles in students). Working in a less-than-desirable setting may be an excellent opportunity to be salt and light as a Christ-follower.

> *I'm gratified to learn*
> *from Scripture that*
> *all work matters to God.*

If your work is less than fulfilling, appreciate that you receive a paycheck. Remember the widows in Ouagadougou, and give thanks as you deposit your earnings and pay your bills. As a person alone, add to your lifestyle a rewarding volunteer piece to give you that "aha" sensation at the end of a tiring day. I'm gratified to learn from Scripture that all work matters to God; He is neither impressed by great-sounding job descriptions and titles, or dismissing of the everyday tasks of life.

If you are facing changes, challenges, even dilemmas related to employment, you are not alone! Our statistics shared in chapter 3 on finances show that a widow's needs are reduced to 80 percent of her previous income. However, her income typically becomes 63 percent of her income as part of a married couple. That gap between 63 percent and 80 percent does not go away. It is not surprising that employment and income become important in our new life pattern.

Some choose to change lifestyles and/or relocate rather than look for more income. Thankfully many of us have choices. E-mails I receive at my ministry tell me that this is difficult when there are children at home and in school. Relocation is not without hardships. As with other big decisions, we always encourage waiting two years, if possible, to make those big decisions, and consulting with your wise board of directors throughout the process. For most widows, employment has an impact on our personal mission. Few have the luxury to start with a blank slate and do whatever we dream of doing. With that fact as a given, we practically access who we are and the necessities in our current life. From this, we create our mission statement.

THE BENEFITS OF CREATING
A PERSONAL MISSION STATEMENT

What are the benefits of having a mission statement? There are many.

- ◆ When choices are necessary because our life is feeling cluttered, holding an activity up to the light of our mission statement helps us choose what to discard.
- ◆ We set boundaries for time, emotional, and financial investment. Seldom does this happen without us declaring some investments "enough," "no more," and "the end."
- ◆ We add new aspects to our life and discard others because we are no longer reacting, but initiating based on our values and what we treasure.
- ◆ We are free of the yardstick others may apply to our life, the "how can I please you?" measure. Why? Because we have carefully determined our mission with accountability to our Creator.
- ◆ We are at peace about what we did not accomplish. It was not our priority when compared to our mission statement.
- ◆ We are free of comparisons with other people. Questions like "Who is most productive?" or "Whose accomplishments are more valuable?" become irrelevant. Our missions are simply different.

Let's go back to the question we asked at the beginning of this chapter: "Will I have purpose in my new life as a widow?" I trust you can say now with assurance, *yes*. That purpose, given the reality of your Creator in your life, is your mission. Parenting, employment, or ministry may be our continuing purpose. Or something totally new and amazing may emerge.

Will each of us see that in those early days after our loss? Probably not. It may take months for our mission to be clear. For some, mission will appear with clarity given the demands of life at the time. For others of us, we search, ponder, and decide. For most of us, we welcome something positive to do with those new empty hours. I trust that the exercises and questions of this chapter provide a framework and a productive time of helping you focus on your new life ahead.

History to mystery to mission becomes our welcome journey of hope. Patches of history, like pieces of cloth for a new quilt, are fit together in our one-of-a-kind new life. We never imagined it could be so beautiful. What at one moment seemed like disconnected scraps becomes interesting, comforting, and useful. We have a mission.

Now let's look at our new faith.

Chapter Ten

A New Faith:

God Moves from Good to Grand

—⊙⊙⊙⊙—

"To reach the port of heaven, we must sail sometimes
with the wind and sometimes against it—
but we must sail, and not drift, nor be at anchor."
—Oliver Wendell Holmes

*I*magine with me for a moment. Imagine that you have lived alone for a bit, and now the following things have either fallen into place, or you have managed, wrestled, planned, or guided them into reality. Your checkbook is now balanced. You know your resources and have created a way of living within those resources. For some, that is a big leap of imagination as we are still sorting and making changes, seeking new sources of income, downsizing—whatever it takes. If you needed a new or different job, you have found it. If you needed new skills to get that job, you have done so. Resources in and resources out match.

Imagine that your monthly calendar has settled into a comfortable balance of activities with new friends, and also activities and connections with old friends. Old friends are those who, by your mutual actions, show you are still important to each other. The things you do and the connections you keep hold you in a comfort zone, balancing your loneliness with a sense that others still care for you. You have moments of feeling alone, but they do not overwhelm you.

Imagine that your daily routine works for you. You awaken with a sense of purpose for the day. You sense that your priorities match your mission in life. The rhythm of your schedule works for you. You have a reasonably healthy lifestyle. You no longer sense confusion over the unknown in front of you. Yes, tomorrow is never guaranteed, but to the extent that the daily decisions are yours, you've made wise ones.

Imagine that you are at peace about your family tree. Notice, I did not say you have the ideal family tree, or even a great or good one. I said *you are at peace* with your family tree. If there were no children as a result of your marriage, you accept that. If your adult children are struggling with their own loss, if they're at odds with you, or not getting along with one another, you've set a boundary around your worries and are not struggling to fix everything. If your children make poor choices, you keep silent or advise appropriately. You have let go and are at peace with the realities of life as it is today in the family tree.

KEEP IMAGINING

Is your imagination getting maxed out? I understand. I have been on this journey almost two years as I write this. Just today I discovered the additional amount I need to budget monthly for federal taxes. (Yes, it took two tax filings as a single person for those numbers to emerge.) And I write huddled in Bob's big soft shirt for comfort, having just finished my umpteenth cup of coffee with a Hostess chocolate cupcake. I haven't arrived. We're all imagining here, right?

Imagine that your emotions are no longer dictating your sleep pattern, what stores you can enter, or the kinds of music to which you can listen without crying. Imagine, in other words, that your emotions have settled in to a new part of your existence where they can invigorate or energize you, and give you a sense of empathy for others. You still feel deeply, but you are not immobilized by the intensity of grief, anger, loneliness, or fear. Just imagine.

Your connection to the organization (probably church) that represents your belief system is settled and comfortable. We know that many have made a change in which organization that is, and some perhaps have separated themselves from any organization. But you have contemplated this carefully, and have arrived at a comfortable and appropriate place for you.

> *I do not believe that we face death as we have without a profound change in our faith.*

If all those things were true, would this describe the new you? Not quite. I believe there is another incredibly important part of each of us that is never the same. I do not believe that we face death as we have without a profound change in our faith. Regardless of the size and strength of our faith before, regardless of the foundation of our faith, I believe that faith is never the same. I can address this change from my experience. But it is not my unique experience alone. Daily, literally, through my ministry, e-mails, media interviews with people calling in, and meeting with groups, people who have experienced profound losses state emphatically that their faith has changed. Again, I can say, "I understand. Me too!" Let's look at how and why this happens. And then let's look at the possible outcomes.

A PLACE WE CANNOT GO

To face death in the one with whom we've shared daily living, our bodies, souls, and minds, the very air that we breathe, is a profound experience. Whether death came suddenly, slowly, from understandable causes, or beyond comprehension, each of us has touched the end of life as we knew it. Our intimate companion, the one with whom we shared ups and downs, days we treasure and those we regret, has gone to a place we cannot go at this time. We cannot peek in, we cannot hear, smell, taste, or touch the new existence of our mate.

Who can experience death so close up and not hunger to know more of this "other world"? We now know of a power beyond anything human. Death demonstrates that power. There are no scientific

formulas, no historic books, no humans in any age who can make
sense of this. While medical research can document and predict
much, we see the greater reality that life's end, and what follows it,
is a mystery.

We may have experienced the death of our parents, siblings, or
even a child. And all of these brought us up close to death. The exit
of our mate to this other world is profound, perhaps more so, than
any other loss we experience. (One exception might be that of a
child. We expect them to live longer than we do. I have not experienced such a loss, and cannot fathom the profound pain of it.) I do
know we are all forced to ask the question, "What's next? Where
are they? What are they doing?"

Have you tried to imagine life after earth? If you are a Christ-
follower, as I am, you may have read Scripture that describes this
next life. Its location: heaven. Books are written, some based on
Scripture and some on fanciful imaginations. I have heard songs,
like "Finally Home," that are so poignant and real that I feel I can
run my fingers through heavenly sand on that shore—and I'm not
even sure there's a sandy beach there! (If there is, surely a catamaran waits for me, and I can invite Bob on a delicious ride, showing
him my new skills with sail and rudder!)

If you are not yet a Christ-follower—or if the Christian faith is
new to you—you may have researched other books that describe
life after this. Many spiritual advisors and leaders have much to say
about this next life. Usually their proclamations are geared toward
requiring certain behaviors in this life to earn whatever rewards are
available ahead. Be sure that when you choose books on spiritual
subjects, you're choosing material that is biblically based and not
fanciful or even false.

Whatever our foundation of faith, I believe every widow's mind
examines that future as we never have before. It's not uncommon
that, after our human mind tries to imagine the life our mate now
has, we run back to the familiar. The reality of this other life is beyond our finite minds. I hug Bob's shirts. I gently remove the cap of
his aftershave and breathe deeply. I huddle on the floor in the last
place I held him. I try to drink in the reality of the man I knew and

touched. This other world is beyond my contemplation. I must rush for comfort to what I know, what my humanness can remember.

But our minds go back to that other question. What is the reality of life after this?

But our minds go back to that other question. What is the reality of life after this? Let me just encourage you by saying that while your/our questions may be troubling and sad at times, the search is a good one and can result in knowledge quite worth the sad moments. While each of us must search for ourselves, may I offer the truths I have discovered?

While many other spiritual leaders claim great powers and rewards for following their instructions, only One stated He would conquer death; He would die and come to life again. That leader was Jesus. He left evidence that His statement was true: an empty tomb. Based on that reality, I determined He is the only leader worth studying, the only One whose answers matter. All the other leaders I studied had statements about life after death, but no experience of living that life to back their claims. If they could not speak from their own life after death, their comments are theories, not reality. Theories do not satisfy my mind or comfort my heart. Only real truth can do that.

I encourage you to search for truth about life after this one. My highest recommendation is Scripture. Here are some truths we can know from Scripture.

- ◆ While our bodies return to dust, our spirit returns to God (Ecclesiastes 12:7).
- ◆ At death, the human spirit goes immediately to heaven or hell (Luke 16:22–31, 23:43; 2 Corinthians 5:8; Philippians 1:23).
- ◆ We determine where our spirit will go based on our acceptance or rejection of Jesus, God's Son (John 3:16).

- ◆ While our actions *illustrate* our acceptance of Jesus as God's Son, our actions do not *earn* us the right to enter heaven.
- ◆ Heaven is an excellent place.

There are many more references about this other world. Entire books are written on the subject, so I won't elaborate here. My purpose is simply to say, in the spirit hunger you are experiencing as a widow, there are rich answers to be discovered in your search. Feed your spirit hunger by learning. There's great comfort in the recognition that while the person we loved is no longer with us in the physical reality, his spirit lives on. For Bob I know that place immediately was heaven. While Bob was still here, I did not have a high motivation to learn of heaven. Scripture wisely says (Matthew 6:21) that where your treasure is, there will your heart be. My treasured Bob is there in heaven now. I've been motivated to study this next place, and that study has been rewarding, invigorating, and comforting. I wish that awesome next place for everyone to be heaven.

NEW MEANING WHERE WE ARE

Who can face death and not undergo a profound examination of what we believe about this life? What's worth living for, and what is, or is not, worth dying for? Who can wrestle with the "why him," "why us," "why in that tragic way"? The endless list of questions trip over the battered-down fences into our brain, and repeat themselves in new ways and with new intensity. As our numbness wears off or we learn new facts about the circumstances, we ask, "Why?" I have yet to know or hear from a widow who has not asked at least some of these questions, if not all.

When I refer to the battered-down fences into our brain, my description is inadequate. But I think you know what I mean. In those early days, we put up a fence around our brain, as it is too painful and scary to let those questions in. Our fence may be superficial at first. "I neither need nor want to know. I'll think about that later. And, meanwhile, I'll find other pursuits to fill my brain. No room for that now."

The fence cannot last forever. Eventually those questions enter and must be answered. Like the icy fingers that entered around the windowpane of my cold attic, you cannot forever keep the questions out. To whom do we take the questions? We can ask other people. They have opinions, but no answers. No one could answer my question, "Why did Bob contract amyotrophic lateral sclerosis?" No medical formula can explain the beginning of life or its ending. No great philosopher can answer all the questions we ask. History books can teach us about human nature, wars, and the reasons for the rise and fall of empires. But there is no explanation for the transition from this life to the next.

Some people thought they were addressing the questions I had in my mind. Many offered their opinions, thoughts, and favorite verses without my asking. Usually those people liked their own answers but were clueless about my experience. I found only one real place to take my questions—and actually He is a person rather than a place. He is the Creator of life and this earth in the first place. If we knew Him before, we will become better acquainted with Him after our time of questioning. And I can assure you, it is worth the big "Ask."

Even if you must first argue, cry, and even shout your despair and disbelief to Him, it's worth the great debate. He can handle it. I share my personal experience with those questions, not because they will satisfy your different questions, nor do they include a comprehensive theological position. This is merely one person's experience that may encourage you to delve for enough answers to result in good after tragedy in your own life.

MY QUESTIONS

The why of death sorted itself into two categories for me: Why death in general? And why Bob's specific death?

Why death?

The general answer is the easier one for me. God's perfect creation did not include death. Adam and Eve chose to go their own way, not follow God's direction. The result was that sin changed this perfect place. Without that entrance of sin, Adam and Eve would have lived forever. But the result of their not following God's instructions was that God's perfect creation was tainted. His beautiful earth experienced earthquakes, hurricanes, drought, and more. His perfect creation of humanity (Adam and Eve were created in perfection) succumbed to illness and disease, and killed one another in jealousy, hatred, and greed. Genesis 3 describes what happened. The rest of Scripture describes the consequences.

Recognizing that if not for the influence of sin, God's perfect creation would never have experienced death, my mind is no longer susceptible to the cruel statement we often hear when we are grieving our loss. Quite commonly we hear someone say to us, "God is sovereign. He decided to take him or her." That individual then may say, "He understands. Go to Him for comfort." Why would we go for comfort to the One who caused death?

Remember, death was not God's master plan. God did not invent suffering. In fact, He is a good God who does not delight in your suffering. His loving heart breaks as ours breaks. Illness and tragedy, which resulted from human rebellion narrated in Genesis 3, is not His ultimate desire for us. His heart breaks when we hold a dying child, a child whose purpose will never be fulfilled on this earth. His heart breaks when He sees one of His created people hounded by pain as life leaves their body. His heart breaks as He sees us grieve, letting go of one we wish to hold on to. This is the God of all comfort into whose arms we can rush for comfort. This is the One we can go to for help.

Reports of real life permeate Scripture. Both New and Old Testament are filled with accounts of people who sinned as did Adam and Eve. People suffered the consequences of sin in their lives and on this earth. Also, stories are told of people who suffered consequences they did not deserve. Stories of overcoming, of faith through everything, are woven through each chapter.

I can accept the reality of death in general. God had a plan. Even as humans chose sin, and death entered the world as a consequence, God's perfect and ultimate plan was revealed in Jesus. In the person of Christ we see the holiness and compassion of God and experience the paradox of death: God can comfort us. He can heal our broken hearts. So my first question of "Why death?" is answered. It is allowed, but not without hope.

Why this specific death?

The specific answer is more difficult. Some widows do not ask that question. I admire their simple faith. Or is it actually profound acceptance rather than simple faith? I don't know. I can just say for me, I did ask God, "Why? Why Bob? Why ALS? Why at such a meaningful and productive season in his life?" You may skip the next several paragraphs if you prefer, as they are personal. I realize that each of our journeys and questions are unique. I include mine in case anyone might benefit from my dialogue with God over my loss. Here are the answers, as I know them today.

God did not invent ALS. He has allowed disease; He did not author it. As we said earlier, God did not intend for any of His created people to experience illness and death. These were consequences of the entrance of sin into the world. Bob and each one of us are susceptible to tragedy because of that. Innocent children die, good families' homes burn, innocent people are imprisoned. Not God's intentions. But this is earth, not heaven.

> *I pondered all this and still could not make sense of it. In my questioning, prayers, anger, and frustration, God gave me two answers.*

God can prevent and direct anything. He does not always do so. In my experience, He usually does not intervene to miraculously cure illness, though He can. He does not miraculously intervene in corrupt court cases to ensure justice, though He could. This kind of sovereignty is difficult to understand and harder for me to accept, especially when terrible things happen to people I love. However, I see it as truth illustrated in Scripture, seen in this world as I have observed it, and real in my own life experiences.

ALS entered Bob's body for an unknown reason. He did not have the hereditary type that is predictable, but the kind that attacks anyone. Just as the treatment and cure are unknown, the reasons it enters certain people and how it does so is unknown to humans at this time. This illness was not deserved or a result of sin in Bob's life. While he would have never seen himself as a spiritual giant, nor claimed to be so, he was a good man. By standards in Scripture, he honored his father and mother, attempted to live by godly standards, was a caring husband and father, and a man of integrity in his work and life. From my 24/7 observations and many promises in Scripture, he deserved a long, healthy, productive life. It would have been fair. But that did not happen. God allowed this wicked disease—in some ways more terrible in an active, athletic person, a man of great energy and vitality.

I pondered all this and still could not make sense of it. In my questioning, prayers, anger, and frustration, God gave me two answers. There is no reason He needed to answer me at all. I count it grace, mercy, and undeserving love that He did so.

One answer was that there are mysteries I will never know about God's work on this earth. He can and will let me know some good outcomes from the very terrible illness Bob suffered. But there are battles beyond my sight and understanding of which Bob's battle with ALS were a part. "For our struggle is not against flesh and blood, but against the rulers, against the authorities, against the powers of this dark world and against the spiritual forces of evil in the heavenly realms" (Ephesians 6:12). " 'For my thoughts are not your thoughts, neither are your ways my ways,' declares the Lord" (Isaiah 55:8).

It would be unfair of me to call Him my God, and then require Him to think and reason like I do. I would have to live a lie to accept His sovereignty and then require that His acts compute with my human brain. It would be hypocritical to call Him Lord, and expect Him to run His plans through my grid of influence and advice giving before He, Creator and God of the universe, could act.

In summary: His answer to me for why ALS in Bob was this: *Dear daughter of Mine, in this life you will never comprehend why.*

In every sense, this will be a mystery from your standpoint. It requires that you simply trust Me.

The second answer comforted my troubled heart, and did make some sense to this limited human mind. God allowed me to glimpse good that resulted from Bob's witness *because* of his terrible illness. Professional colleagues, friends, and family respected him through his life for his faith and integrity. But I can just imagine a discussion in heaven (similar to what happened with Job). The Evil One appears before God's throne and states something like this in his grating, raspy, accusatory tone:

"Of course, he lives an obedient life. His parents loved him. He accepted Your calling. He has family and friends. Okay, so his job is stressful, not always easy days; his wife and kids are ordinary on their good days. But You've allowed worse for Your followers. He obeyed Your call because he was healthy and he loved what You called him to do. Lift Your protective hand, and I'll throw something in his world that will make him bitter, and wipe that big smile off his face. Then we'll see the transparency and depth of his devotion to you." And God lifted His protective hand, because He knew He could trust Bob: his heart, his faith, and that his smile was real from the inside out, not dependent on good things in this life.

The last chapter of Bob's life on this earth resulted in his talking to others with the same disease about his faith and his guarantee of heaven. In the ALS support group meetings, others sometimes entered the room with a bitter heart and understandable anger. But they left with a real, up close and personal encounter with a man suffering equally, and yet was fully at peace with life and death.

His professional colleagues saw a stronger faith in their friend; because the cruelty of the illness was obvious, while Bob's joy and optimism was greater. He declared to individuals in private and to thousands from stages and over airwaves that he knew his tomorrow and was at peace. His question for them was, "Do you?" On Easter Sunday of 2005 he said to the thousands in several services, "Not long ago you saw me ushering right in this aisle. Now you see me in this wheelchair. I know I'll be in heaven soon. But some of you in this room will die before I do. Are you ready?"

I could not lift his motionless hand back into his lap, strap his four-hundred-pound wheelchair into our van, lift the straw in his glass of water to his lips without marveling myself at his courage, and seeing people visibly changed by experiencing Bob—with ALS. From spiritual leaders in our country to yesterday's visit from our landscape specialist, I continue to hear of the impact of his life in those months and years of illness. So I spend the words to write this, trusting that you might see that good we cannot imagine does happen. Would I have willingly offered my Bob to ALS for the witness? My weak faith and human love must admit, no. But there are many things in this life to which I now say, "We don't get to pick; yet good things can happen from bad experiences."

> "*It* has changed my priorities,
> what I live for, what I want
> to be remembered for."

And I can say as well that I have seen great, unexpected glory going to the God he loved during my husband's illness. Bob showed me how to live for what he believed in—no matter what. My friend Joyce (as I write this, it is the third anniversary of her husband's exit to heaven) put into words our experience. "We contemplate their lives and decide what was important. It has changed my priorities, what I live for, what I want to be remembered for." Well said, my friend. We grasp new meaning in our lives recognizing how temporary we are. We tend to think there will always be a tomorrow, tomorrow to pick up the pieces of a disaster we created today. To pay off the debt for the item we charged, because we could not delay gratification today. To apologize for the bitter words we should have swallowed, rather than spit out today. Tomorrow is not guaranteed. Today is what matters.

What are our choices?

Our faith has changed. The ground we stood on has shifted. We realize that life as we know it is not forever. We can choose to let our questions push us to learn and understand God at a different level and with fresh commitment. We can choose to let our glimpse of a world beyond this be our springboard for stronger faith. Or we can choose to let our shaking world shuffle us into a corner of stagnation. We can detach from the spiritual moorings we had because we don't like the waves we've had to endure. Let's compare the outcome of these two options.

Option number one: We learn new things. We read, we learn, we pray, we explore, and we get some answers about what matters. Our minds are stimulated and refreshed with our new discoveries. We discover that God, while still beyond our understanding, does engage with us as one person, one questioning person, one hungry person for new truth. We trust Him with a new tenacity, because for one reason, no one else comes close to having understandable, reasonable answers for all the questions we raise. With our new baby steps of faith, there is a surprise companion: a spirit of optimism, hope, a belief that tomorrow might be brighter. And indeed it often is. Like the wind at my back on the catamaran. Like counting the twenty-two deer on my neighborhood walk. Like hearing my grandchildren refer to their grandpa, whom they only had for a few years. (They were adopted into the family shortly before he became ill.) Moments like this one I will describe are evidence that this new life has incredibly real and love-filled moments.

Edmond, my youngest grandson and now twelve years old, recently commented that he was sorry Grandpa only heard them play their instruments when they were all so bad. In their school system, instrument selection and lessons start in the fifth grade. So, shortly after Bob's diagnosis, after Albert had had only a few lessons on the trombone and Edward equally few on the tuba, and Edmond had had no lessons yet on the trumpet, Valerie and Mark assembled them in our living room to play everything they knew for Grandpa. What can I say? I know of no adequate adjectives to describe the concert.

What different musicians they are today! Edward has played in the Palmer House Tuba Christmas concert. Edmond is first chair trumpet. Albert, following in Grandpa and Uncle John's tradition on the trombone, would make him so proud. My response to Edmond is that Scripture (Hebrews 12) tells us there is a cloud of witnesses cheering us on in this life. I think Grandpa is firmly in the cloud watching and listening to their musical progress. We imagined him not only hearing their concerts, as he could have done here, but now their practice sessions and rehearsals too. He can encourage them in any moment they think of him. He was able to tell each of them his pride in their future and love for them. This grandpa is still cheering them on!

Faith in God's Word brings that huge hope, makes a smile break out at their remembering him, even as my eyes leak a bit. What happens if we choose to abandon faith because of these rough waters? We are left to trust a tomorrow dependent totally on our human resources. We must be our own god in our life. Power and resources for our future must come from within us. And most of us, at this time, realize our own weakness and vulnerability as we never did before. There is not much basis for optimism in this scenario. One might argue that the widow blessed with material wealth, health, and lots of friends might be content and hope filled. If that were true, and not all such widows are content, that leaves out the majority of us who simply do not have all that external good stuff in this life. I have talked to women who have rejected faith temporarily, but courageously came back to question and discover a new and more sustaining faith.

Which option attracts you? The one that invites learning, produces hope, and gives us options of worthwhile reasons for living? Yes, that option requires faith, but offers solid foundations on which to base that faith. Or the one that leaves us to settle in and stagnate with what we believed before. No new hope to grow and anticipate the unknown, no new vision for our tomorrows. I trust your answer is that you will embrace stronger, more grounded, more empowering faith than you have ever experienced before.

From my experience, this new faith does not give you back what you miss so terribly of your life before. But you will be comforted beyond measure. And your new faith will be loaded with new gifts and blessing that are precious though different. You will see God's hand in what others see as coincidence, but you have a clearer discernment of how God works and how up close and personal He is in your life. You see Him clearly when He is invisible to others. You have empathy for other people who would have been invisible to you before. You have strength to reach out to others struggling in hard circumstances because your muscle for life has been strengthened through your own rough times. You have hugs and sometimes words for those whom others avoid in discomfort. You have a new future of caring, tenderness, and opportunity, all powered by your new faith. As a new woman, with a new mission, you have a new power.

It's called faith.

Appendix A

A Special word
about Children at Home

————⟨∞⟩————

 *M*any thanks to the bold parents who have given me permission to share their stories here. At the conclusion of this section, a summary will highlight specific helps that can be gleaned from their experience.

Marie is a recent widow with eight children. She writes that her teenage son is a very angry young man who has become verbally abusive to her and the other children. She wondered if anyone else has dealt with a similar situation and can give her some advice?

My response to Marie:

My dear Marie. Sounds like you are in for quite a growing experience in your faith and parenting. I am checking in with a widower, a dad with teenagers, who might be able to give you a male perspective and counsel. Meanwhile, here are a few things I know. You must establish yourself as head of the household, because that is what you are, though not by choice, I know. As head, you determine acceptable language standards. Violating that brings consequences. What consequences is your son receiving? If they are not working, what consequences will? I don't know how you can share this with your son, but two truths are essential.

1. Anger is an appropriate emotion given the loss of his dad.

2. Being rude and disrespectful is not an acceptable way to get rid of anger.

Often physical activity helps get rid of that anger/ adrenaline thing. However, I do not know your son, and that may or may not be a place to start. Maybe he can help decide with you what he can appropriately do when he is angry.

My prayers are with you today. God's strength and blessings to you.

Marie responded:

I'm not doing very well at establishing myself as the head of the household. I've always been the weaker parent: more indecisive, emotional, hesitant to "lay down the law." How do I become the head of the household?

My response:

A good thing is that you know yourself as you are. This is a real beginning and God will help you from there. I'm sure it is your desire to be Christlike. Remember that Jesus was a leader, strong and focused. You can become that, because that is who you must be now with your children. Deciding your family goals so that you prioritize where you invest your energies as a parent is a good place to start.

Marie responds:

I don't have any goals right now, other than trying to make it through each day without having a nervous breakdown! Obviously, the most important issue is the kids' spiritual lives. I try to have Bible reading and prayer time with the kids each night at 7:00 and feel that I have accomplished something if we get this done. (Sometimes, the older kids have evening activities: sports, debate, etc., and we don't have our devotions.) So if spiritual training is the most important thing to me, how does this become our family goal? What would our home look like with that as our goal?

"E-mail dad" writes (Yes, this is lengthy, however, it is price-less, and so worth reading!)

Miriam forwarded your e-mails and asked if I'd be willing to offer a "male" perspective. It is my prayer that these thoughts may be of some assistance. I fully agree with what Miriam has already written about the need to "vent" and release anger and pain. I've sensed and seen this in my own daughter, and the need has been confirmed in our lives by counselors as well. So I don't, or at least try not to, overreact when my daughter goes into the backyard and cusses out God at the top of her lungs. God can handle it. Hopefully the neighbors won't call the police. It is only by going through this, by releasing the pain and anger inside of her that she can go on to the healing parts of grief. Profanity in casual conversation is another issue altogether, and my daughter is experimenting with that as well. Whenever I hear it, I correct it immediately. I remind her it is inappropriate and unnecessary. It violates the standards of our family. I don't use such language and she is not allowed to either. What I see is my daughter both being a teenager . . . testing her limits and boundaries . . . and reacting to grief. I find it is almost impossible at times to separate the two.

My daughter's response to grief I understand as well. In the biggest crisis of her life, no one, not me, not family, not teachers, not the church—not even God—saved the life of her mom. In her mind we're not reliable. She has stated that she's going to do things on her own. She doesn't need God or anyone. And then she promptly gets into trouble . . . and doesn't understand why. I approach her needs, fears, and doubts with a threefold attack. We are body, mind, and spirit. No one can heal themselves. Believing that God uses doctors as well as pastors, I've gotten psychiatric care for my daughter. If she had broken a leg, I wouldn't hesitate to go to the hospital; well, there is a physical component to our thoughts and emotions.

Mentally I support my daughter via counseling. Even psychiatrists recognize the limits of "pills." "C" needs help thinking the right things. An experienced counselor helps her with perspective. My daughter doesn't like going, and I always end up doing most of the talking, but by the end of the hour she is talking on her own. It seems everybody has advice and wants to talk to my daughter. I severely limit this to protect her, but there are a few that I "insist" she talk to. The alternative for her is being committed to a psych ward, and that's enough to make her talk.

Most important, I support my daughter spiritually. She regularly visits with one of our pastors and his wife. Also my daughter and I are reviewing Scriptures that lay out God's relationship and His love for her. I routinely pray with her and for her. I try for the evening devotions, but most of the time what I'm able to do is recognize and capitalize on teaching moments. These are those moments in everyday life that I can tie back or attribute back to God. We've recently had very interesting discussions on angels started by a seemingly innocent question asked in the car.

No surprise to you, boys are different. Makes you appreciate the "fearfully and wonderfully made" part of Scripture. Not to mention the idea that God has a sense of humor. Before you get too smug, remember us guys think the same about you women as well. My recent experience of losing my wife has made me really cognizant of my need for strength in my life. I think it is common among men. We are drawn to strength. Kinda explains football, pro wrestling, NASCAR . . . We are God-wired to bear burdens, but in doing that are often overwhelmed and need to know that someone out there is strong enough. Strength comes from strength. We vicariously tap into the strength of others. Ultimately that person is God, but we men tend to look for it in each other first. Originally we look for it in our dads. It isn't lost on me that at the point your son needs it the most, you are least equipped to offer it. On a good day you're probably not the strength a fourteen-year-old future man is looking for, and today is not your good day. As someone has wisely said, God knows what your son needs. It is not by accident that He has written that He is "a father to the fatherless." Other men in your family's life will be used to step in to represent the strength that God provides. As your son matures he will learn to go direct to the source himself.

A woman on a Christian radio broadcast once detailed how she wasn't drawn to the "Big God" of the Old Testament, the One who did big things like creation and miracles and making nations, but she was more impressed by the God who became small . . . in the person of Jesus . . . and cared about the little stuff of day-to-day life: water from a well, sickness of a child, hunger. The emphasis for her was on love and relationship. At the risk of stereotyping, most men are drawn to that "Big God." We need to know that the One who placed within us the urge to bear burdens and provide support to others is bigger than the problems we constantly experience and see. Again, strength comes from strength. Men are often drawn to the God who spoke and life began, who empowered man to halt the sun, split rivers, who can rain down fire from heaven when need be. We think plagues are cool. Imagine, cut me off on the freeway; I drop a swarm of locust on your pristine lawn. Yeah!!! The man who can model strength and confidence for your son will have appeal to him. A Christian man will recognize and acknowledge that this strength comes from THE FATHER. The source of all strength. This isn't about being a tough guy or macho. It is about being the man God wants your son to be and to become.

This is starting to sound preachy and I'm not qualified to do that to you. I'm a fellow Christ-follower, a widower and single parent these past eleven and a half months, and I pray for you and your family.

Marie writes one month later

"R" has been better lately. I had a very serious conversation with him about a month ago and really laid down the law. I told him that his behavior has got to change or I will find a group home for him to move into. Maybe that sounds extreme, but we just couldn't handle the constant verbal and physical abuse anymore. He has been much more settled down since then. I'm so thankful to have connected with you. It's been a good resource for me. Sometimes it's nice just to have someone else to talk to who has had similar experiences.

Marie writes six weeks later

"R" is still a struggle for me. I've decided to get some counseling for *myself* so that I can learn some better parenting skills. I've tried sending him to counseling, but he just sits there the whole time and won't talk.

My response to this courageous mom is, "Applause, applause, applause! Widowconnection.com will continue to pray for you and your family. We especially pray that godly men will come into your son's life to model his heavenly Father. You are becoming a woman and mother of strength. We salute you!"

Summing it up:

◆ You are the head of the household now.
◆ God can and will help you be that.
◆ Pick your priorities.
◆ Remember each child is unique: gender, personality, age, and stage matter.
◆ Capture teachable moments.
◆ Cultivate relationships with other families where dads are willing to relate to your children.

Another young mom with five children ages five to eighteen shared more practical insights for parenting alone.

Susan says:

"The first year had much fun and joy, as well as tears and sadness. Each of my children are so different. One, like me, could enter joy quickly, leave and be sad, and then be on with living. While others, wired up differently took longer to 'recover' from feelings of sadness."

Wisely, Susan knows them and allows them to be different, for them to be real with themselves. "There was such security in knowing that David always had my kids' best interests at heart. If I was skewed or lost my perspective, there was always that other person. Committed, unconditionally, sacrificially, living, breathing for me and for those kids. And now I'm the only one, their number one advocate. Everyone else has their own focus.

"Then I go to the verse, 'I will be a father to the fatherless, a husband to the widow.' I had a dream or vision, you might say; Jesus was in a tuxedo and I was in my wedding dress. Jesus was carrying me across a threshold—exhilarating, exciting, wish-filled. I did not see His face but He had me; I felt Him saying to me, 'I'm your husband; you are where I want you to be. I will be with you in this house, raising these children; this is what I designed for you.' Might not be my design, but it's His.

"I go to the verse, 'Pour out your heart like water to the Lord and lift up your hands on behalf of your children' (see Lamentations 2:19, the theme verse for Moms in Touch). I go on to Lamentations 3:21, 22, and 23. He has called me to be their mother and He will give me what I need to be their mother, but not their God. 'This I called to mind . . . great is your faithfulness.'

"I'm getting to the place of saying not 'what is God going to do for me,' but 'what is He going to do with me?' How is God going to work this out? David was able to verbalize this to God in the presence of his children as they gathered around his bed. "I'm giving them back to You" was David's bold statement of trust.

Susan states today with firm resolve, "This is our opportunity in history to experientially live that God is who He says He is, to

know that God is enough for us. If God is life, then death is completely other than what He is. Death is almost in defiance of Him.
God did not intend for us to die. Yet precious is the death of God's
loved ones. In their moment of dying, He holds them closely in His
heart."

Susan draws intense daily comfort from her faith, what the
Bible says to her, and the biblical foundation her husband laid for
their family.

"What is a day like now?" I asked.

Six thirty in the morning begins the check to make sure everyone has heard their alarms. Now two are in high school, one in junior high, one in grade school, and one in afternoon kindergarten.
Next—lunches. Four lunches and snacks, sometimes two sandwiches for the children in sports, and a snack for the youngest. They
pick their snacks, and of course, all have their personal preferences
for sandwiches. (No wonder Susan frequents the grocery regularly!)
And then the commotion of catching the bus. She has made new
ground rules after the first year. If you forgot it, the consequences
are yours. After a year of much driving for left-behind items, she
decided things needed to change. Her rationale? If the teacher as-
signs it, she believes you can and will complete it and are capable of
turning it in.

And then there are the decisions of who will represent at all the
events? Soccer, volleyball, basketball, golf, and tennis. Susan has
new empathy for single parents and families in which both parents
work outside the home.

I am impressed by her frankness with her children. "I do not
try to be their mom and dad too. I'm their mom." She says she has
told them, "God tells you He will give you what you need. And you
don't have a dad here now. I am only your mom."

She confidently states that her life today is not about her. "It's not
about how strong I am in holding on to Him. He holds me fast. It's
about Him. He won't let me go. He is faithful when I struggle. All I
have to do is fix my eyes on Him. And when I'm too tired to look up
at Him, He cups my chin in His large gentle hand and lifts my head
so I can fix my eyes again on the One who has not failed me yet."

One cannot look in on Susan's life without recognizing that her faith is being stretched, refined, and enlarged as she parents her five children.

Summing it up:

◆ Recognize you cannot be both parents. You can only be you.
◆ Turn appropriate responsibilities over to your children. (Yes, they can.)
◆ Lean heavily on the truths of Scripture for encouragement.

Appendix B
*H*OW TO START
a Widows Group

———⬥⬥⬥———

*M*y applause to you for wanting to reach out! One of the most frequently asked questions coming in my e-mail is "How can I start a widows ministry?" While most of you asking the question are widows, several are not and just care about us! I am going to offer suggestions from four viewpoints:

- A widow who wants to start a group with church support
- A widow who wants to start a group on her own or with another organization
- A person who cares about us and wants to start a group with church support
- A person who cares about us and wants to start on her own or with another organization

In each category, the following are common and vital:

- Prayer is a vital and first step.
- Assess what the needs are of those you want to serve. A survey form is available on my ministry Web site Widowconnection.com.
- Expect to persevere through surprises, challenges, and opportunities.
- Revel in the blessings of obediently serving those close to God's heart.

A widow who wants to start a group with church support

Make an appointment with a church leader, pastor, elder, or deacon. Simply tell them of your interest in starting a group. Depending on the needs of your church, it may be a Bible study, prayer and share time, social outing, or lunch-bunch. Needs are different, and it is important that you find what your widows need. Remember that few, if any, widows are on church leadership teams, and your church leaders may have ideas that simply do not serve or comfort widows. Gently share your experience and help them see how the church can support you in providing for this group.

Our group's meeting format is a two-hour Saturday morning session consisting of greeting, forty-five minutes studying the Bible, followed by breaking into groups of five or so around tables to share, pray, and/or discuss our Bible study topic. Your group may prefer evenings, or have a Sunday school time to meet. Churches usually are eager to include activities in their bulletins, provide coffee, and mail announcements as needed. Groups may choose study materials or create their own. Griefshare.org is a popular resource providing videos and workbooks. Other ideas are social events or prayer. Our group has gone to teahouses and museums, and had game nights. The important thing is not to be overwhelmed by what you *might* do. Simply start doing what you *can* do.

A widow who wants to start a group on her own or with another organization

There are often good reasons to meet in a home, library, or community facility. This may be a better environment to bring friends, or create a group of widows from different faiths and church affiliations. As the leader, you may still state that the underlying orientation will be Christian in nature though any person is welcome. While it may take more effort to create and distribute flyers, local papers may publicize your meetings. Again, determining the needs of the group is key. You will probably be approached by those who want to be guest speakers. Be aware that some may see that as a potential market to sell products—financial, travel, and others. It is wise to have your purpose well outlined to keep the meetings focused on ministry to widows.

A person who cares about us and wants to start a group with church support

While a widow has empathy for other widows like no other, there simply may be no such person to lead such a ministry. If you have a heart to serve, you can be incredibly helpful and have a thriving group. I have a single friend who began a group consisting mostly of widows and widowers. They love her! The group satisfies their need for connection. The material they study is secondary and any topic is fine with them. As we suggested above for a widow starting the group, begin by making an appointment with a church leader. Assess the needs in your church and begin. I offer our format as an example above, but again, provide what your group needs.

A person who cares about us and wants to start on her own or with another organization

While this is a more challenging scenario, I do know of some successful ministries to widows that are neither widow-led nor church-based. If you have a passion to help widows, you will persist through each challenge. My main additional advice beyond all in the above scenarios is to be clear on what you are motivated to provide, and "stick to the knitting," as the old business adage goes. Provide a support group, home repairs, housing, encouragement— the opportunities are endless.

Appendix C
*C*HURCH RESOURCES
and Organizational Model

———⟨∞∞⟩———

*A*ssuming you are in a leadership role and are considering start-ing a ministry for widows, here is a summary of background information. My hope is that you will discover who we are and how we feel, making your efforts practical and real for our needs. While this section repeats information found in earlier chapters, I'm as-suming you may only read this portion, as that is practical for your goal.

Following the background information is a suggested organi-zational model and samples of two forms you may find helpful as you begin.

Who are the widows among you? Eight hundred thousand join our ranks every year. We are a fast-growing demographic noticed by new home builders and a lucrative niche for health and beauty products. We are invited to dinners by financial planners and sur-veyed by designers for home features that will convince us to sign on the dotted line.

In contrast, one pastor described us by saying we moved from the front row of church to the back row of church and then out the door. We moved from singing and serving to solitude and silent sobbing, and then on to find a place we belong. Approximately 50 percent leave the church they attended as a couple. Scripture says the character of a nation is shown by how it treats us; in fact, the character of individuals and the church is shown by how it treats us. Remember those 103 references to us in Scripture that indicate we are close to God's heart.

Who are we? We are perhaps the most invisible among you—the widow. I am one. I am a part of the fastest growing demographic in the United States as baby boomers age. We lose 75 percent of our friendship network when we become one. Sixty percent of us experience serious health issues in that first year. One-third of us meet the criteria for clinical depression in the first month after our spouse's death, and half of these remain clinically depressed a year later. Most experience financial decline.

If someone had described this scenario to me five years ago, I would have stated emphatically, "It can't be so! In the community of believers we support each other. We walk together on the journey." I look back on my own responses to women who became widows and realize how little I understood, how little I empathized, how seldom I walked beside them. Many, in fact, became invisible, whether it was in ministry positions, small group participation, or social events. Of the approximately 50 percent who leave the church they attended with their spouse, some reconnect to a place that matches their needs.

If someone had quoted the friendship statistic, I would have thought, *That won't be me. With the network that surrounds Bob and me, I will never experience loss of that magnitude.* Yet I did. Connections we had that were primarily through our husbands, change; and departures—though inevitable and appropriate—are still painful to process.

May I help you understand us by describing some of my personal experiences? Becoming a widow means *nothing* is the same. With Bob's exit to heaven absolutely every iota of my existence has changed: my calendar, my checkbook, what's in my fridge, the wake-up alarm time, the thermostat, the traffic pattern in the bedroom, which restaurants I can enter, and yes, the look in my children's eyes when they step through the door on holidays. My living space is more cluttered, I seldom use makeup, and I am familiar with the smell of car oil as I sit in Lube Right next to the overdone coffee wondering what Bob did when he waited here.

There are other changes so private and personal they cannot be shared. Loneliness and solitude are words that are not descriptive enough of the space that becomes the cocoon of the widow. We discover that our journeys are very different and we fit in no mold. However, we have an incredibly strong connecting bond that links us to one another because of our shared experience.

What do we have in common? We discover we are vulnerable as never before. We are pressured to purchase products we neither need nor can afford. Salespersons use their influence as our "friend" and even a fellow believer who is looking out for us. We are concerned about our finances. Most of us experience financial decline. Women experience fewer years of employment and less income, which often has a dramatic impact on their preparation for being alone or retired. In my decades as a churchgoer, I have never heard a message on 1 Timothy 5:8 (a passage that admonishes believers to provide for their family) that included appropriate attention to wills, trusts, and life insurance. The likely event that one person in the marriage will exit to heaven before the other brings financial implications that are important to address. While in biblical times God's people were told to take care of the widows and orphans among them, it is assumed now that the government through Social Security and other programs will care for the invisible among us—a theory for which the numbers do not work.

Our emotions change more drastically than the reversals on the extreme SheiKra roller coaster ride at Busch Gardens—a ride I entered ignorantly rather than have my grandsons unaccompanied through the long line. I regretted that ride immensely as a two-hundred-foot drop rearranged my insides. Imagine this contrast. Two become one in marriage. At nineteen years of age I embarked on my journey with Bob that lasted 41 years, 2 months, and 21 days.

Sixteen months after meeting Bob, this nineteen-year-old sophomore who had never been to Chicago or heard of Moody Bible Institute married a man who knew his life calling was to serve God through Moody Broadcasting. Finishing degrees, becoming a city girl after knowing life as a farm girl, moving six times, having children, adopting children, being in church choirs, showing hospitality wherever we lived, and traveling to forty countries together was part of the journey. I became an educator—a teacher and counselor in public high schools for twenty-six years—yes, a working mom. As he followed his calling, he led the MBI network to thirty-six owned and operated stations. He negotiated with the Federal Communications Commission successfully and was able to begin a satellite ministry that at times has served six hundred affiliates. We parented our children to adulthood, which was unquestionably the greatest challenge in our marriage. We enjoyed the marriages of three children and worked and toiled over our home as two chose to have their wedding receptions in our yard. No smile was broader on either Bob's face or mine than watching our three incredibly handsome African-American grandsons grow.

In an incredibly productive season of his life, while serving as vice president of Moody Broadcasting, treasurer of National Religious Broadcasters, and board member of HCJB (Heralding Christ Jesus Birth—an international broadcasting group), Bob fell. The inconvenience and pain of a dislocated shoulder began the journey to doctors through disease, through sorting through our theology, to facing the bleak reality: amyotrophic lateral sclerosis is untreatable, is fatal, and it had gripped Bob's body.

Less than three years after that fall he entered heaven willingly: I gave him up with more than reluctance. Our "one" was now ripped in "two." My inarguably better half was gone, and the gaping wound created by his exit had every nerve ending screaming even though I was supposed to be numb. The ride on the SheiKra was docile compared to this. While every widow's story is different, we all share the common understanding of a loss that is final beyond description. There will be no phone call, no plane delayed but still landing, no second chance to right our past regrets. Sitting curled up on the cold ground watching the gardener gently work the grass seed into the fresh dirt on my husband's grave set me apart forever from the life I once had. Other widows understand that.

What else do we share? We gain a fresh perspective on Scripture.

Second Corinthians 1:3–4 is so relevant. No one can comfort us like another widow. In turn, we are moved deeply when we see another woman enter this experience, and we want to comfort her in her grief. We study the 103 Scripture references to widows with desperation to find whether we are invisible to God as well. With gratitude we discover that we are not only close to God's heart, but He measures everyone by how they treat us (James 1:27). This is both a comforting and sobering insight. Widows, orphans, prisoners—the voiceless—God chooses to speak for us.

He instructs that our needs be met (Deuteronomy 24:17) through the church's tithes if necessary (Deuteronomy 14:29, 26:12; Acts 6:1–4). He instructs that in our vulnerability we be given our legal rights (Isaiah 1:17; Luke 18:1–8). He commends us for our sacrificial giving (Mark 12:42–43). He tells our story—the widow at Zarephath and her generosity (1 Kings 17:9); the widow, her pot of oil, her faith and obedience (2 Kings 4:1–7).

As I studied Scripture on widows these themes emerged:
To the widow:

- Be generous regardless of the quantity of your possessions; no one's stuff is their own anyway.
- Be filled with faith—you can't help but be when you see how special you are to your Creator, who is your new husband.

To the church:

- The significance of your church is not in its numbers but that its priorities match those of God.
- The character of your leaders is not measured by their popularity or power but by their attention and care for the powerless and voiceless among them—widows, orphans, and prisoners.

ORGANIZATIONAL MODEL

How can churches respond to the widow today? The problem is complex for several reasons. First, churches today are varied, ranging from small struggling bodies with limited resources both in staff and financing to megachurches whose staffs are lean and depend on volunteers to minister to most needs other than teaching. Second, the experiences and needs of widows vary widely and there is no one-model-fits-all to be created. *Recognizing that the following recommendations must be adapted to the individual church,* here are some suggestions.

1. Form a leadership group including at least one widow— Scripture is clear that there should be appointed leaders in the body to oversee the care of widows (Acts 6:1–7). The ministry arm might well be done through deacons and deaconesses following the model of 1 Timothy 3:8–13. I would personally add (clearly this is my personal addition) that all leadership groups related to widows' ministry have a leading member who is a widow. Ministry leaders are typically married men who understandably cannot fathom our circumstance. It has been my experience that lacking this leading widow, churches' decisions of how to serve us often miss the mark of meeting the real needs of widows.

2. Survey widows' needs—once the leadership team has been established, determine who are the widows, and then follow up with a survey to discover their needs. A survey is included on pages 205–206 as a sample. While financial needs and help with upkeep of living space are common, need for connection is typical. Remember the 75 percent loss factor? Most connections with the church are broken upon becoming a widow. This time period is the widow's most painful, lonely, and vulnerable part of her journey, a time when she needs believing friends near her.

3. Address the needs as expressed in the survey—some churches already have sources of help in place. Do not assume that a new widow is aware of your household helper team or any other resources you offer. We prepared a referral list on pages 206–207. These are typical needs of widows. Ideally contact will be made with new widows to inform them of your resources.

4. Provide a specific connection for widows to the church—in our Widow to Widow ministry we study Scripture together, share our journey, and do fun things together as well. If your church has only a few widows, you might partner with other churches and provide a seminar day. Widowconnection.com is available to consult with you as you plan.

On my journey as a widow, I have learned that we all change. And much of the change is good. We become faith-filled because we cannot face the day any other way. We become strong because we have no other choice. We are compassionate because our heart has been broken. As I listen to other widows' stories I am awestruck at what they have learned and accomplished.

One of my change points occurred in Africa seven months after Bob's exit to heaven. I traveled to follow in Bob's footsteps to Burkina Faso, a place I had not previously been able to accompany him. I was connecting with believers whom he had assisted in broadcasting. Prior to my trip, I received an e-mail asking me to speak to widows groups there since that was now my reality. "Of course." In one season of my life I had taught Bible studies, and my interpreter would be Bob's friend. This would be a way for me to give back while walking in Bob's footsteps.

The result: I spoke to seven groups of widows comprised of twenty to two hundred women. I spoke in one church service where the men were the predominant note-takers. I spoke to one assembly of five churches, which I thought would be a group of widows. (I quickly sorted my notes from the widow and her pot of oil to the transitions in Joshua's life.) I delivered my message with five pastors sitting behind me in large impressive chairs. After listening intently to my teaching, one pastor issued their pronouncement: "It is good."

I can only say simply, I was changed. I remembered Bob's encouragement to me to accept my first speaking engagement after my first book was published. I was hesitant. He said, "Honey, they want to hear the person behind the book." So I went reluctantly. This was different. A different woman emerged in Ouagadougou, Burkina Faso. With an open Bible and hungry learners in front of me, I was energized and embraced the opportunity.

Yes, we have changed. As we get acquainted again you'll discover that we believe Romans 8:28 with a new tenacity. We have
new and relevant gifts to offer not in spite of, but rather because of
our loss. We are bold because we have already faced death in a part
of ourselves. We laugh at things many people fear and count blessings among the mundane events of an ordinary day. Invisible? Let's
change that. Welcoming the widows reflects the heart of God. Ministering to the widows among you brings a double blessing. We are
strengthened to give back, and the body of believers is rewarded
for obedience. Bless you as you move forward with this important
work!

QUESTIONNAIRE FOR WIDOWS

Name _____ Date _____

Address _____

Home phone _____ Cell phone _____

E-mail _____

Years of being widow_____ Age _____

Ages of children _____

Do you attend this church?_____

What is your greatest need?_____

_____

What is your greatest fear?_____

_____

How can we help you?_____

_____

Would you be interested in events for widows?

Rank preference, 1—low, 5—high.

_____ Discussion group

_____ Bible study

_____ Social events at church like game nights or crafts

_____ Social outings off campus

_____ One-time seminar of resources

Names and addresses of other widows who might benefit from this ministry

_____

_____

_____

_____

What topics would you like for us to include in our studies and discussions?

_____

_____

SAMPLE REFERRAL LIST   **Date compiled**   (your church logo)

Include name and phone contact for each referral. If church number, include extension.

Get permission from each resource to list them.

NOTE: Assume there are costs unless noted otherwise or the church has predetermined they will cover the cost.

Attorney/estate probate/trust/will/real estate transaction

_____

Auto repair/tires

_____

Benevolence at your church

Cars ministry

_____

Financial information

_____

Food pantry

_____

Home maintenance

_____

Biblical Counseling Center

_____

Carpenter/handyman

_____

Computer help

_____

Counseling (through your church)

_____

Electric

Financial Advisor

Financial Counseling

Church financial counseling resource

Trained Crown Financial counselor in your area

Heat/air/furnace

Insurance agent

Roofer/painter

Plumber

Windows/siding/roof

Appendix D
$\int$EVEN TIPS
for You to Help Widows

---⌒∞⌒---

1. **Please do stay connected.** There is already a huge hole in our universe. Do not assume we need space to grieve.

2. **Please do say you are sorry for our loss.** We would rather you tell us you do not know what to say than tell us your story of losing your friend or even close relative We may be able to listen to your story later, but not now. Do not tell us you understand.

3. **Do call and ask** specifically, "Can we go for a walk to-gether? May I run errands for you? Meet you for coffee?" Do not say, "Call me if you need anything."

4. **Do refer to our husband's acts or words**—serious or hu-morous. We are so comforted by knowing our husband has not been forgotten. Do not leave our husbands out of the conversation.

5. **Invite us to anything.** We may decline but will appreciate being asked. Do not assume we no longer want to partici-pate in couples events.

6. **Do accept that we are where we are.** Marriages are brief, long, healthy, dysfunctional, intense, remote. Death comes suddenly or in tiny increments over years. Again, our expe-riences are so different, as are we. So is our journey through grief. Do not assume we go through the outlined grief process "by the book."

7. **Walk the talk.** Do not make "conversation only" offers such as "We'll call you and we'll go out to dinner"—and then not follow up. Yes, we are sensitive in our grieving, but we'd rather hear you say, "I've been thinking of you" than make an offer just to say something.

Appendix E

Seven Holiday Tips
for Those Who've Experienced Loss and Those Who Love Them

1. **Please say, "I remember."** We love to hear tender, funny, and just interesting things from your perspective.
2. **Let go of your expectations**: yourself and others.
3. **Be willing to flex from traditions.** Changes are not necessarily permanent and things will be different anyway.
4. **Guard your heart from your ears.** You will hear people say things that you shouldn't take personally.
5. **Prepare for the unexpected**, both positive and negative. Remembering a favorite dish that does not need to be prepared, an item that needn't be purchased, an empty chair, will occur when we least expect it.
6. **Make a memory.** For example, for Christmas, create an ornament with the person's name and a word that describes them, or simply a picture.
7. **Try something new**, lighthearted, and fun.

Appendix F

FINANCIAL HELPS

⸺⧞⸺

Crown Financial Ministries has given me permission to copy their forms here for your information to illustrate the paper/pencil method. You may download them from my Web site Widowconnection.com and create your own "workbook" by making copies and stapling them in a manila folder to create your own 12-month workbook.

Let's walk through the paper-and-pencil method. Here is one simple recording tool.

| Month | Year | | **Monthly Budget** | | | | |

Category	INCOME	TITHE/GIVING	TAXES	HOUSING	FOOD	TRANSPORTATION	INSURANCE
BUDGETED AMOUNT	$	$	$	$	$	$	$
Date							
1							
2							
3							
4							
5							
6							
7							
8							
9							
10							
11							
12							
13							
14							
15							
This month SUBTOTAL	$	$	$	$	$	$	$
16							
17							
18							
19							
20							
21							
22							
23							
24							
25							
26							
27							
28							
29							
30							
31							
This month TOTAL	$	$	$	$	$	$	$
This month SURPLUS/DEFICIT	$	$	$	$	$	$	$
Year to Date BUDGET	$	$	$	$	$	$	$
Year to Date TOTAL	$	$	$	$	$	$	$
Year to Date SURPLUS/DEFICIT	$	$	$	$	$	$	$

BUDGET SUMMARY

This Month
Total Income $ _____
Minus Total Expenses $ _____
Equals Surplus/Deficit $ _____

+

Previous Month/Year to Date
Total Income $ _____
Minus Total Expenses $ _____
Equals Surplus/Deficit $ _____

=

Year to Date
Total Income $ _____
Minus Total Expenses $ _____
Equals Surplus/Deficit $ _____

Monthly Budget

Category	DEBTS	ENT./REC.	CLOTHING	SAVINGS	MEDICAL	MISCELLANEOUS	INVESTMENTS	SCHOOL/DAYCARE
BUDGETED AMOUNT	$	$	$	$	$	$	$	$
Date								
1								
2								
3								
4								
5								
6								
7								
8								
9								
10								
11								
12								
13								
14								
15								
This month SUBTOTAL	$	$	$	$	$	$	$	$
16								
17								
18								
19								
20								
21								
22								
23								
24								
25								
26								
27								
28								
29								
30								
31								
This month TOTAL	$	$	$	$	$	$	$	$
This month SURPLUS/DEFICIT	$	$	$	$	$	$	$	$
Year to Date BUDGET	$	$	$	$	$	$	$	$
Year to Date TOTAL	$	$	$	$	$	$	$	$
Year to Date SURPLUS/DEFICIT	$	$	$	$	$	$	$	$

Let's assume you have copied the forms and created your folder. Keep it in a convenient place. Take a few minutes each day and write down any money you spend. Record checks written for utilities, rent or mortgage, and even that cup of coffee. Simply record in the date box coinciding with the category the dollar amount you spent that day. (If this is too basic for you, count yourself blessed, and skip to what you need.) Here is a sample of what your records might look like.

MONTHLY INCOME AND EXPENSES

GROSS INCOME PER MONTH _____
- Salary _____
- Interest _____
- Dividends _____
- Other (_____) _____
- Other (_____) _____

LESS:

1. Tithe _____

2. Tax (Est. – Incl. Fed., State, FICA) _____

   NET SPENDABLE INCOME ═══════

3. Housing _____
   - Mortgage (rent) _____
   - Insurance _____
   - Taxes _____
   - Electricity _____
   - Gas _____
   - Water _____
   - Sanitation _____
   - Telephone _____
   - Maintenance _____
   - Other (_____) _____
   - Other (_____) _____

4. Food _____

5. Automobile(s) _____
   - Payments _____
   - Gas and Oil _____
   - Insurance _____
   - License/Taxes _____
   - Maint./Repair/Replace _____

6. Insurance _____
   - Life _____
   - Medical _____
   - Other (_____) _____

7. Debts _____
   - Credit Card _____
   - Loans and Notes _____
   - Other (_____) _____
   - Other (_____) _____

8. Enter./Recreation _____
   - Eating Out _____
   - Baby Sitters _____
   - Activities/Trips _____
   - Vacation _____
   - Other (_____) _____
   - Other (_____) _____

9. Clothing _____

10. Savings _____

11. Medical Expenses _____
    - Doctor _____
    - Dentist _____
    - Drugs _____
    - Other (_____) _____

12. Miscellaneous _____
    - Toiletry, cosmetics _____
    - Beauty, barber _____
    - Laundry, cleaning _____
    - Allowances, lunches _____
    - Subscriptions _____
    - Gifts (incl. Christmas) _____
    - Cash _____
    - Internet _____
    - Other (_____) _____
    - Other (_____) _____

13. Investments _____

14. School/Child Care _____
    - Tuition _____
    - Materials _____
    - Transportation _____
    - Day Care _____
    - Other (_____) _____

    TOTAL EXPENSES ═══════

INCOME VERSUS EXPENSES

- Net Spendable Income _____
- Less Expenses _____
  ═══════

LIST OF DEBTS

as of _____

To Whom Owed	Contact Name Phone Number	Pay Off	Payments Left	Monthly Payment	Date Due	Interest Rate

FINANCIAL STATEMENT

as of _____

ASSETS   LIABILITIES[4]
  Liquid Assets[1]   _____ $ _____
  _____ $ _____   _____   _____
  _____   _____   _____   _____
  _____   _____   _____   _____
  _____   _____   _____   _____
  _____   _____
  Total Liquid Assets $ _____   **TOTAL LIABILITIES** $ _____

  Invested Assets[2]
  _____ $ _____
  _____   _____
  _____   _____
  _____   _____
  _____   _____   NET WORTH $ _____
  Total Invested $ _____   (Assets-Liabilities)

  Use Assets[3]
  _____ $ _____
  _____   _____
  _____   _____   TOTAL LIABILITIES
  _____   _____   AND NET WORTH $ _____
  _____

  Total Use Assets $ _____
  TOTAL ASSETS $ _____

[1] Cash, Savings Accounts, Checking Accounts
[2] IRAs, TSAs, 401(K)s, Investment, Real Estate, CDs, Antiques presented at fair market value.
[3] Residence, Autos, Personal Belongings presented at fair market value.
[4] Outstanding Real Estate Loans, Credit Cards, Auto Loans, Personal Loans.

Appendix G

STUDY INFORMATION

$\mathcal{P}$lease visit Widowconnection.com for chapter-by-chapter material for *From One Widow to Another* suitable for individual study or group discussion.